The
BURRELL
COLLECTION

New Edition

With an Introduction by
JOHN JULIUS NORWICH

 HarperCollins *Publishers*
in association with
Glasgow Museums

Glasgow|museums

This book illustrates more than 300 of the 8,000 objects
in The Burrell Collection. As a result of changes in
displays as well as reasons of space and conservation
requirements, it cannot always be guaranteed that an
object illustrated or discussed in the book will be on display.

The sizes of the objects are indicated in the captions in *cm*
(centimetres) and *in* (inches). Where no dimension is
given, the first figure refers to the height of the object and
the second to its width.

To aid the reader who wishes to use the book in the
gallery, a colour code system has been used to identify the
different areas of the Collection. A plan of the building
and a key to the colour code are given on the back cover of
this book.

First published 1983
Revised reprint 1984
Eighth impression 1992
New edition 1997
Reprinted 2001, 2006, 2010
Published by HarperCollins Publishers
© Glasgow City Council (Museums)
ISBN 0 902752 55 3
ISBN 978 0 902752 55 9

Design, Editing and Photography: Glasgow Museums
Architectural photography: Keith Gibson
Index: Patricia Bascom
Cartography: Mike Shand

Printed in Great Britain by Scotprint

The
BURRELL
COLLECTION

HarperCollins Publishers
and Glasgow Museums
acknowledge the generous help of

Clydesdale Bank PLC
in the preparation of this book.

Contents

Introduction John Julius Norwich

On the occasion of his visit in 1983.

Let there be no mistake about it: in all history, no municipality has ever received from one of its native sons a gift of such munificence as that which, in 1944, the City of Glasgow accepted from Sir William and Lady Burrell. The paintings, sculpture, tapestries, ceramics, stained glass, furniture, silver, metalwork and *objets d'art* of every kind, from three continents and virtually every period, which together comprise the collection that bears his name, leave one spellbound – not only for their quality, but also for their quantity and the quite astonishing breadth of taste that they represent. Apart from the fifty or so paintings that have adorned the walls of Kelvingrove Art Gallery, and a relatively small number of other masterpieces that have accompanied them to occasional Arts Council exhibitions, most of these items have spent the past four decades crated away in storerooms, waiting in dusty darkness until they could be given a permanent home. Now, at last, that home is ready for them, and the full magnitude of Sir William's achievement – and of his generosity – is revealed to the world.

He was a born collector. Not many boys start buying paintings in their teens – and fewer still if they have the sort of father who is cross because they did not buy a cricket bat instead. And of these few, how many are still at it when they are 96? Eighty years of continuous collecting is surely quite a record in itself, particularly when pursued with such relentless determination as Sir William invariably showed. His final total of some eight thousand objects means an average of about two new acquisitions a week during that entire period; and most of those acquisitions, it should be remembered, were preceded by days (and occasionally even weeks and months) of studying catalogues, consulting experts and haggling with dealers. This last occupation, it seems, was a particular favourite of his: true to his origins, there was nothing he loved better than stalking his prey. No collector ever drove harder bargains, or

was more familiar with the Byzantine intrigues of the sale room, or was more respected for his acumen by the trade. Admittedly, his methods were not invariably successful. There were occasions when, while Sir William bided his time, a rival moved in and snatched away his bargain. There were others when he just could not bring himself to bid the extra thousand or two that would have secured him a masterpiece. But the fact remains that, over the years, he got infinitely better value for his money than any of his major competitors. It was only seldom – very, very seldom – that Sir William Burrell was sold a pup.

He bought not only copiously but over an incredibly wide range. It would not, perhaps, be altogether true to say of him, as of Browning's "Last Duchess", that he liked whate'er he looked on, but his looks certainly went everywhere, and I can think of no other private collector – not even among the Rothschilds – with a comparable catholicity of taste. He was, on the other hand, no magpie. All good collections, however varied they may be, must reflect the personality of their collector, and Burrell's is no exception. He was, first and foremost, a traditionalist; he had no time for the avant-garde. In painting, he tended to stop at Degas, in sculpture at Rodin. This is not to say that he did not occasionally venture a little farther – there is a ravishing Cézanne landscape and even a rather unexpected Epstein bronze – but it is no use looking for a Derain or a Giacometti. Secondly, he liked colour and form rather than delicacy or elegance; of all the centuries between the 11th and our own, it is the 18th that comes off worst. Where he was quite remarkably ahead of his time was in his appreciation of the artistic – as opposed to the archaeological – value of prehistoric civilizations; there is a terra-cotta lion's head, dating from about 1800 B.C., that lingers long in the memory.

And yet, however superbly other periods

may be represented in his treasure house, it was clearly the Middle Ages – at any rate where European art is concerned – that Burrell loved the most. His collection of stained glass, with at least one item going back to the 12th century, is probably the best and most comprehensive to be found anywhere outside a major cathedral; his tapestries, too, bear comparison with the best that the world's museums have to offer. And there are some medieval church treasures that still have the power to catch the breath: the little Romanesque Temple Pyx, for example, a tiny bronze mount representing three sleeping soldiers covered, Brunnhilde-like, by their long kite-shaped shields; an enamelled *châsse* depicting the murder of Thomas à Becket and doubtless fashioned soon after the event; a tomb effigy of a recumbent Spanish warrior from a church near Huesca, its original colouring almost intact; and an early French Gothic Virgin and Child, carved in boxwood, that regularly moves visitors to tears and would do the same to me if I were fortunate enough to live with it.

Most of these pieces, and countless others, I first saw in the storerooms while workmen were still hammering away above our heads on the pedestals and plinths and showcases that were to be their permanent home. One by one the treasures were lovingly lifted from the cupboard shelves and carefully divested of their plastic wrappings and their tissue paper; a marvellous Tang camel; a late 14th-century Ming ewer, decorated with a copper-red underglaze, of staggering beauty; a celadon bowl from Korea which I was told was easily worth a quarter of a million pounds and consequently did not dare to touch; from Egypt, a 6th-Dynasty relief of a boy carrying a goose; from Rome, an exquisite little mosaic of a cock with long, irregular tesserae giving the sweep to its tail. And these came from only one or two of the cupboards; scores more, containing who knows how many other hidden miracles, remained tantalizingly unopened. At the end of one long row, the Collection's chief restorer worked patiently away with a tiny stick tipped with cotton wool, cleaning the hairless pate of a large Chinese ceramic figure representing a disciple of the Buddha, seated, in corpulent serenity, on a rock.

But great works of art are not made for store cupboards, and the City of Glasgow deserves something rather more than three rousing cheers for having, at considerable but totally justified expense, provided the Burrell Collection with a setting worthy of it. Mr Barry Gasson's new gallery is not the least of the masterpieces awaiting the visitor to Pollok Park. What an inspired stroke it was to place it, not in the middle of that broad green meadow, but up against the woodland edge! The trees outside dapple and diffuse the light; the architect can therefore construct his long northwest wall almost entirely of glass, making the natural setting an integral part of his scheme and contriving, with the occasional glorious vista through a long enfilade of rooms, to link the real woodland with the fabled forests of the tapestries and even with the stained glass beyond. How cunningly, too, he has achieved unity without monotony, keeping the same display system throughout – this is, after all, one man's collection – but using stone showcases where the floors are of stone and, where they are carpeted, wooden ones that echo the marvellous roof of laminated Russian pine.

But all this is to anticipate. The Burrell-Gasson experience begins for the visitor as he approaches the entrance, which incorporates in its smooth, pinky-red Dumfriesshire stone the first of several Romanesque, Gothic and Renaissance portals and window-openings that Sir William bought, when already in his nineties, from William Randolph Hearst's great collection. From here he is led forward by a distant vision of another, still greater, portal – from Hornby in Yorkshire – to a broad, glazed court set with wild fig-trees but dominated by the mammoth Warwick Vase from Hadrian's Villa at Tivoli, a recent acquisition by the Burrell Trustees. Just what Sir William would have thought of this somewhat alarming object must remain uncertain, but he would certainly have felt at home in the rooms that line the court on three of its sides. These are faithful replicas of the three principal rooms in which he lived at Hutton Castle near Berwick-on-Tweed, with their own furniture, linenfold panelling and – most impressive of all – the dazzling stained glass with which he adorned them. The tall, early 16th-century panel from the Rhineland, depicting Joachim and Anna embracing in front of the Golden Gate, is one of the *pièces de résistance* of the whole gallery.

Emerging on to the long northwestern side, we find ourselves at once among the more exotic items of the Collection: the Egyptian, Greek, Etruscan, Mesopotamian and Assyrian, followed by the Japanese and Chinese. These then give place to Medieval Europe and finally – at the far northeastern end – to the paintings which continue down the eastern side. Those of the 15th and 16th centuries come first: thus it is the Cranach of Cupid complaining to Venus about his bee stings, the Giovanni Bellini *Virgin and Child,* and the Memling Virgin of *The Annunciation* (what would we not give to have the other half of it, with the Angel Gabriel?) that will blaze out through the glass walls of the gallery, offering an invitation to enter that only a barbarian would be able to resist.

Despite the evidence of one of the best of Rembrandt's self-portraits – a youthful one, formerly in the French royal collection – and a Frans Hals which, at £14,500, was the most expensive item Sir William ever bought, he seems never to have been in real sympathy with the art of the 17th and 18th centuries; and so we pass on to the pictures he loved best – those of 19th-century France. One or two of them, it must be said, let the side down a little – his admiration for Monticelli is nowadays a little hard to understand, and there is a perfectly awful late Courbet of a beggar giving a coin to a small boy – but the balance is redressed by no less than ten ravishing Boudins and similarly superb displays by Manet and Degas, including a picture of a ham by the former, which the latter kept in his study. Among the surprises, I remember most clearly a prancing grey horse by Géricault – only a sketch, but painted in a metallic, gold-dusty symbolist style almost in the manner of Gustave Moreau – and a wondrously evocative Millet pastel – *L'Hiver aux Corbeaux* – which seemed to encapsulate the whole of Normandy on a late November afternoon. I have kept till the last the greatest jewel of them all. It is Alfred Sisley's *The Bell-Tower at Noisy-le-Roi,* and for it I would willingly sell my soul.

This last group provides a salutary reminder of an important fact which we Sassenachs tend to forget: that in the past it has been the French rather than the English who have provided the predominant influence in Scottish cultural life. It should be no surprise to us, therefore, to learn that towards the end of the last century Glasgow was one of the best markets for French paintings outside France itself, and the home of not one but several distinguished and highly knowledgeable dealers. Of these, the most important was Alexander Reid from whom Sir William acquired several of his best pictures. From our point of view it is a pity that the superb portrait of Reid by Van Gogh – with whom he had actually shared an apartment in Paris – is not part of the Burrell Collection. But we cannot really complain: it hangs only a short distance away among the treasures of Kelvingrove which owes the sitter, I suspect, an even greater debt.

The picture gallery ends with the Hague School and, among the prints and drawings, with selections from his vast hoard of works by two of his contemporaries, Joseph Crawhall (who deserves to be better known) and Phil May. But we have still confined ourselves only to the periphery of the building; what, you may ask, of all that lies at its heart – the Tapestry Gallery arranged like a medieval Great Hall, with armour and weapons and the suggestion of an Elizabethan parlour beyond? The late Tudor and early Jacobean needlework collection, second only to that of the Victoria & Albert Museum? The Japanese prints and Islamic prayer rugs, the Rhineland glass and the Queen Anne Silver, the ivory and the alabaster and the treen?

All this, alas – and much else beside – must be left to more learned pens than mine. My only object has been to try to give the reader some hint of the pleasure and the sheer excitement that awaits him in what is surely the most important new museum to have been built in Britain since the South Kensington complex over a century ago. I have, in concluding, only one major regret: that there is no portrait of Sir William Burrell hanging in the great building that bears his name. But this was his express wish; it was, he used to say, the collection that mattered and not the collector.

Perhaps, after all, he needs no further memorial.

Sir William Burrell

The Burrell Collection was given to the City of Glasgow in 1944 by Sir William and Lady Burrell. Sir William Burrell (1861-1958) was a wealthy Glasgow shipowner with a lifelong passion for art collecting. The family was of Northumbrian origin, and his grandfather George moved to Glasgow in the early 1830s. By 1856/7 George was established as a shipping and forwarding agent at Port Dundas, the Glasgow terminus of the Forth and Clyde Canal. In the following year he was joined by his son, Sir William's father, and henceforward the firm traded under the name of Burrell and Son. Initially its shipowning was confined to vessels small enough to transit the Canal, but in 1866 it took a half-share in an ocean-going steamer and by 1875 a further six steamers had been built for them. Two bore the prefix "Strath", which continued to be used by Burrell and Son throughout the firm's existence.

In 1876, the future Sir William entered the firm at the age of 15, and on his father's death in 1885 he and his eldest brother George took over the management. Burrell and Son was already prospering, but under their shrewd direction it reached a position of international standing in worldwide tramping and in ship management.

The Burrell brothers undoubtedly had the Midas touch. George kept abreast of developments in marine engineering while William specialized in the commercial side. Their fortunes were based on a steady nerve, foresight and breathtaking boldness. The formula was quite simple. In times of depression they would order a large number of ships at rock-bottom prices, calculating that the vessels would be coming off the stocks when the slump was reaching an end. Burrell and Son was then in a position to attract cargoes because it had ships available and could undercut its rivals. Then, after several years of highly profitable trading, the brothers would sell the fleet in a boom period and lie low until the next slump occurred, at which point the cycle would begin again. It sounds easy, and Burrell himself described it as making money like slate-stones, but none of

the firm's competitors was bold enough to take such risks.

The operation was repeated twice on a large scale. In 1893/4 twelve new ships were built for the fleet of Burrell and Son at a time when the industry was in a very depressed state. A few years later, advantage was taken of the current high prices obtainable for shipping and every vessel flying the Burrell house flag was sold. After going into semi-retirement for several years, in 1905 William and George rocked the shipping world by ordering no fewer than twenty steamers; a further eight were delivered in 1909/10. After a few years of prosperous trading the brothers once again decided to capitalize on the rise in the market values of ships, a rise which became dramatic after the outbreak of the First World War. Between 1913 and 1916 almost the entire fleet was sold, including vessels which were still on the stocks. With his share of the proceeds shrewdly invested, William Burrell devoted the remainder of his long life to what became an all-consuming passion, the amassing of a vast art collection.

By now, Burrell was one of the most important collectors in Scotland. His interest in art went back to his youth. While still a boy he was already buying pictures, although he used to say in later years that their chief value lay in the frames. Although it is not known what sparked off Burrell's love of art, there were plenty of opportunities in late 19th-century Glasgow for him to form his tastes. A number of collectors were to be found amongst the wealthy Scottish industrialists and shipowners of the time, men like Alexander Young, Arthur Kay, W. A. Coats, T. G. Arthur and Sir Thomas Gibson Carmichael. This market was created and serviced by several discerning dealers, of whom the most important was Alexander Reid (1854-1928) who in 1889 opened his galleries in Glasgow. Although Reid stocked works by Monticelli and the Hague School artists, he also gradually introduced Scottish collectors to French painters like Boudin, Fantin-Latour and Degas. In addition, he was a great friend of Whistler and an admirer of

Sir William Burrell

Constance, Lady Burrell

Crawhall. Burrell, many years later, paid glowing tribute to Reid's influence: ''He did more than any other man has ever done to introduce fine pictures to Scotland and to create a love of art.'' Burrell bought from him continuously from the 1890s into the 1920s.

An estimate of Burrell's early interests can be obtained from his loans to the Glasgow International Exhibition of 1901, when he was the largest single lender with more than two hundred works. Their range and scope show that he was already a collector of major standing. They included medieval tapestries, ivories, wood and alabaster sculpture, stained glass and bronzes, Roman glass, 16th and 18th-century Dutch, German and Venetian table glass, silver, furniture and Persian rugs. The pictures numbered amongst them works by the Maris brothers, Couture, Géricault, Daumier, Manet, Monticelli and Jongkind, in addition to two Whistlers, three Crawhalls and seven drawings by Phil May. It is noteworthy that most of the areas in which Burrell collected throughout his long life are well represented, demonstrating that the shape of the Collection was already formed.

Between 1901 and 1911 little is known of Burrell's collecting, apart from his acquisition of some fine pictures, including his first Degas. Unfortunately, at the same time he was selling as well as buying, a policy he was to continue even after the sale of the fleet had removed any major financial restrictions on the scale of his spending on art. In 1902, for example, he sent nearly forty pictures for auction, and among those sold were paintings by Daumier and Manet which are now in the United States.

From 1911 until 1957 Burrell kept detailed records of his expenditure in twenty-eight school exercise books. He made almost all the entries himself, except during the last few months when failing eyesight compelled him to delegate the task to others. These purchase books are an invaluable record of the astounding range and scale of his collecting. Although the entries tend to become more detailed as the years go by, the basic format was established on the first page of the first book. There are separate columns for date of acquisition, description, from whom the item was acquired, its price, date of delivery,

Two pages from Sir William Burrell's purchase books

insurance and whether photographed. The last column is headed "All in Order" and usually has Burrell's initials.

For the first five or six years after the commencement of the purchase books he confined his acquisitions almost exclusively to Chinese ceramics and bronzes, fields in which he appears to have shown no interest prior to 1901. Until 1915 his level of expenditure was low, consisting of an annual average of £500. From 1915 the graph of Burrell's spending starts to rise, coinciding with the sale of the bulk of the fleet. From then onwards, using the interest from his investments, Burrell spent very large sums. Altogether, between 1911 and 1957 his outlay on new acquisitions averaged £20,000 per annum. There are two peaks: in 1936 when his expenditure reached nearly £80,000, and 1948 when he spent in excess of £60,000. His most costly purchases were paintings and tapestries.

Throughout his long career as a collector Burrell bought from many dealers, chiefly in London and Paris. Amongst them was a small number of specialists who acted as his tried and trusted advisers and agents. These included Alexander Reid for pictures, Wilfred Drake for stained glass, Frank Surgey and Frank Partridge for furniture, John Hunt for medieval and Elizabethan furniture and *objets d'art,* and John Sparks for Chinese art.

Burrell was never an easy client. He was strong-minded, liked to haggle over prices and could be very cautious. Even dealers with whom he had done business over some years would find him seeking a second opinion on an object they were attempting to sell him. Burrell was also very circumspect in his approach to a potential acquisition. He liked to "circle round it", as he put it, in order to disarm potential rival bidders if the item were to be auctioned or avoid raising the price by alerting a dealer to his interest. On occasions his refusal to pay high prices caused him to miss some very important pieces, but on the other hand his knowledge, excellent memory and good eye enabled him to pick up some outstanding bargains. It must also be noted that although Burrell was wealthy, he was not in the league of great American art magnates like Widener, Walters, Kress, Mellon and Hearst; in order to compete with them he had to use his resources carefully.

There can be no doubt that Burrell bought extremely well. He succeeded in forming a major collection in almost every field in which he was interested. The Chinese ceramics and bronzes are surpassed only by those of three or four other museums in the British Isles, of which two are national collections, and the Persian, Caucasian and Indian rugs and carpets can be ranked with the holdings of the Victoria and Albert Museum in London. Burrell's paintings, particularly those of the French 19th century, would grace any major gallery. And all this is before the real strength of his collection, the Late Gothic and Early Renaissance works of art from Northern Europe, is taken into account. The entire range of medieval artistic activity is represented: the stained glass stands comparison with the holdings of the Cloisters museum in New York and the Victoria and Albert Museum; the tapestries rank amongst the world's finest collections; and the medieval sculpture, particularly the English alabasters, and the furniture include some outstanding pieces. Taking the medieval section of the Burrell Collection as a whole, it is no exaggeration to say that within the British Isles it is second only to that of the Victoria and Albert Museum in its range.

Until about 1930 Burrell seems to have been buying merely for his personal enjoyment, with no thought of forming a collection which would be kept together after his death. Until then he continued to sell or exchange paintings, but in the 1930s he formed the idea not only of having a permanent collection but of handing it over to public ownership. Burrell had discussions with a number of interested parties regarding the disposal of the Collection, and eventually, in 1944, it was donated to Glasgow, the city of his birth and centre of his business activities, in the names of himself and Lady Burrell. By this time it numbered some 6,000 items. A few years later he gave the then Glasgow Corporation £450,000 for the construction of a building in which the Collection was to be housed and displayed. The terms of the Deed of Gift as regards this building, however, presented difficulties. Burrell stated that it should be within four miles of Killearn in Stirlingshire and not less than sixteen miles from the Royal Exchange in Glasgow. He felt that the Collection would appear to best advantage in a rural setting and was also deeply concerned at the harm which could be caused by the high levels of air pollution then prevailing over Glasgow. The councillors and Corporation officials were aware of the problems in, firstly, finding a suitable site and then in administering a museum so far removed from the city, but attempts to persuade Burrell to make his conditions less stringent met with little success. Various sites were considered, but the issue was still unresolved at the time of Burrell's death. It was only nine years later, in

1967, when Mrs Anne Maxwell Macdonald presented Pollok House and estate to the City of Glasgow, that a site was at last found.

Whilst the search for a permanent home for his Collection continued, Burrell applied his organizing ability to the recalling of those items on loan throughout the country and the transference to Glasgow of the objects in his home at Hutton Castle in Berwickshire. Also, despite his advanced years, his taste for new acquisitions remained undiminished, and the Collection grew at an even faster rate: between 1944 and 1957 a further 2,000 items were added to the original gift. For some years Burrell continued to use his own money for new purchases, but in 1949 he came to an arrangement with the Corporation whereby he was empowered to use some of the interest on the sum he had given for the new museum. In these last few years he continued to buy in the same fields as before, but concentrated on certain areas which he considered needed strengthening. Between 1947 and 1957 the largest number of acquisitions were made in the ancient civilizations of Mesopotamia, Assyria, Egypt, Greece and Rome, a field into which Burrell had scarcely ventured prior to 1944. He felt that these purchases would serve to round off the Collection.

He also kept an eye open for items which would enhance the appearance of the new museum. Some major acquisitions of stained glass were made, especially the splendid series of early 16th-century heraldic panels from Fawsley in Northamptonshire, which Burrell tried to obtain before the Second World War and which finally entered the Collection in 1950. Most important of all was the purchase from William Randolph Hearst's collection of a series of medieval stone doorways, windows and niches, and of screens and other architectural fittings in wood, all of which were acquired with the aim of incorporating them into the fabric of the proposed gallery. It must have given Sir William Burrell much pleasure to know that the Fawsley glass and Hearst Collection items were amongst the best bargains he ever obtained in more than eighty years of collecting. Sadly, he did not live to see them in the gallery in Pollok Park, where they form such an important feature. He died at Hutton Castle on 29 March 1958, at the age of 96.

Notes on the Building **Barry Gasson**

The commission for the building was awarded through a two-stage architectural competition in 1971, and it has taken fully the intervening twelve years to design and construct. Yet, had a national postal strike not caused the first-stage entry deadline to be extended, this design would never have been submitted.

The sense of intrigue felt at the beginning of the project still exists. How does one display a stone portal, once a doorway and now a piece of sculpture, once outdoors and now indoors? What is a piece of stained glass that once had a specific location and message, and now is history to be preserved forever? How does one display objects of one epoch in a building that denies many of the qualities of that epoch? How can the objects that are very explicit be related to a building that tends not to be; and how can the visitor experience these objects, when of necessity protection from light and touch intervene?

The brief for the competition required a building in which to exhibit Sir William Burrell's Collection in Pollok Park, an estate originally belonging to the Stirling Maxwell family, some five miles southwest of Glasgow city centre. It was to be a home for the Collection, where it could be displayed for all to enjoy and experience, but also where these remaining records of civilization could be preserved for future generations.

Architecture is an art. Its form and meaning are directed by essential needs, and to a large extent the quality of a finished building is a reflection of the clarity with which those needs have been described. In the case of the Burrell Collection, for the authors of the brief it must have been an extremely difficult task to assimilate the extent and variety of the Collection and convey these to non-observers, as all the competitors were – yet they succeeded. The message of the Collection was made clear and its dimensions tangible. It is to be hoped that these qualities are now part of the building.

To assist in comprehending the Collection, Glasgow Museums and Art Galleries organized a representative exhibition at Kelvingrove at the time the brief was circulated. Later, during the second stage of the competition, the Collection stores were opened to the competitors, and even if no further success had occurred that would have been a reward in itself.

The Collection was described by what it contained, by its varying degrees of importance and by how much space was likely to be required for its various parts. This space had to be regulated as, for comprehension and for cost, the entire Collection could not be on display at one time. Storage, therefore, and ways of rotating the objects had to be planned. It was also required that a means of easily viewing a succinct portion of the Collection should be made possible while still enabling those with the inclination to spend more time to explore the remainder.

Within these general directions, there were items of special note and of significance to the planning of the building, such as housing the three Hutton Castle Rooms, replicas of Sir William's own rooms at Hutton Castle; the vast size of his collection of tapestries and stained glass; the value of the Chinese and Ancient Civilizations' collections and of the paintings and drawings.

Apart from the display and storage of the Collection, there were the ancillary requirements for a restaurant, a lecture theatre and schoolroom, study rooms, a library, offices, conservation studios for textiles, ceramics, stone, wood and stained glass, a photographic department, general workshops and stores, a kitchen, and plant rooms for all the services. Throughout every part of the building the quality of light and air had to conform to all current practices on conservation. Accessibility also had to be considered. Visitors would arrive by car or on foot, from the park itself, from nearby Pollok House or from the city. The whole field in which the building is now situated was available for use.

It was clear that this was a major Collection,

The Burrell Collection, exterior.

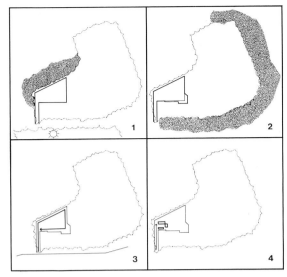

1 *The woods to the north;* **2** *the open field;* **3** *a perimeter route;* **4** *the three Hutton Castle Rooms.*

of great significance to Glasgow. Yet the intentions of the brief were that the building should not be an institution but rather a home in scale and in sympathy with the Collection and the environment of the park.

The design grew from some basic ideas. The first, and the most important, was that this was to be a Collection in a park, not in a city. This offered the opportunity of making the grass, the trees, the woodland plants, the bluebells and bracken, a context for the display of the Collection. It was a delightful place, evoking associations with the time and place in which many of the objects were created, with the traditions of craftsmanship, reflecting that innate relationship between art and nature with which such objects are imbued.

These thoughts suggested that the building be placed alongside, and close to, the trees in the lower corner of the field. The trees – mature chestnuts and sycamores – faced south and were surrounded by rich undergrowth. That aspect of the building facing north would be shaded, and by using glass for the wall an intimate connection would be provided between the woodland grove and the gallery spaces. This north edge eventually became part of the primary route around the building. It is the "walk in the woods", and visually the woodland is linked to the tapestries at the centre of the building.

The second consideration was to resolve the problems posed by the elements of the Collection: how to incorporate the three Hutton Rooms, the stone arches and windows, the timber screens and ceiling, the tapestries and stained glass, the paintings, carpets and many objects of stone, metal and ceramic.

The Hutton Rooms were to be reproduced and furnished as they had been while Sir William lived in Hutton Castle. They were to be a mark of his personality in the new building. These rooms were essentially interiors, yet they had an exterior; the walls were part inside and part outside, part stone and part plaster; the windows had natural light, yet they had also to become objects themselves in the Collection. The solution has been to place the rooms, necessarily out of context, around a glazed courtyard which offers light and an opportunity to show them

The South Gallery looking east.

in their actual state, to be viewed from without as well as within. They are in an important position because of what they are and because they represent in their contents the bringing together of such diverse parts of our culture. They are a valuable contribution to the Collection and to the building.

The stone arches and windows were architectural features and are treated as such here, to be walked through or looked through, yet they are also pieces to be used as sculpture. Their scale and distinction firmly directed the character of the building, its

The southeast corner above the restaurant.

The main entrance to the Burrell Collection building.

The apex of the building from the picnic area in Pollok Park.

shape and form, and the material out of which it has been built.

Two arches in particular were planned to be together, the outside entry arch and the large portal in the Courtyard. Both arches are from Hornby Castle in Yorkshire, where they were the gateways to its courtyard and to the great hall beyond. They are carved from an outcrop of multicoloured sandstone. They were an important consideration in the choice of the pink sandstone for the walls in which they are set, but not before a search had been made for the quarry, albeit now extinct, from which

Hornby Castle was built. The other arches have been located for reasons of place or context. One Romanesque arch heralds the Early and Late Gothic parts of the Collection, another set of small arches overlooks the Tapestry Gallery.

The stonework is permanent and forms part of the building fabric. The large timber elements of the Collection – the Beaudesert Screen and the Bridgwater Ceiling – could be more easily manipulated to make enclosures or create character. The ceiling provides the setting for a medieval domestic interior, and

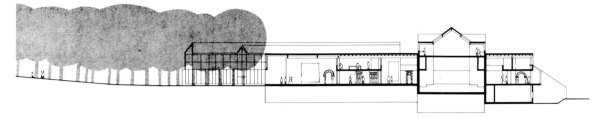

Section of the building from north to south.

the screen forms a connection between the tapestries and the needlework collection.

The tapestries and stained glass are major elements in the Collection. The tapestries required walls, a hall, a space to "warm", that was protected from daylight yet could be made part of the outside woodland scene. The stained glass, on the other hand, required bright direct light and an architectural context. The solution was to hang the tapestries in the centre galleries of the building where they would be visually related to the woodland edge of the North Gallery, while the stained glass panels have been placed between timber mullions along the south side of the building, extending to include the restaurant. The restaurant itself provides an appropriate setting to display the large sets of 16th-century armorial glass.

The requirements of the textiles, paintings and drawings, and the objects of ceramic, metal and stone suggested the need for a variety of other spaces with different light or different size, and for the whole there would be an awareness of the changing seasons and the changing day.

The third basic consideration in the design of this building was that the Collection is extensive and varied, and required a means by which it could be comprehended. A perimeter route was conceived to offer a line of reference around which different elements of the Collection could be arranged. A selection of the major pieces is displayed on this primary route. The perimeter is connected by two cross-routes, partly in the form of daylit galleries, which offer short cuts, aid orientation and enable all parts to be seen as one whole. At the centre of these routes are a gallery for exhibitions and a lecture theatre.

Across the North and South Galleries, the Mezzanine accommodates study areas and offices. The conservation studios occupy the roof space, the plant rooms the basement, and the whole is connected by a central core of lifts and stairs. In a place of its own, halfway

around the building and overlooking the fields, is the restaurant.

Fourthly, as only part of the Collection would be shown at one time it was necessary to plan for flexibility and change in the organization of the display. Yet in respect for the objects, to display them properly it was felt that the building should express authority and permanence. Therefore, rather than design a building that would change for the objects, it was decided to accommodate this need by providing within the building a variety of place, of finish, of location, each with different qualities of natural and artificial light. In this way, it was hoped that certain places would suggest themselves as locations for certain objects, and that the semi-open plan would create juxtapositions that are both intentional and a surprise. In a sense, this would also reinforce the idea of the building being a home as well as an exhibition.

The materials chosen for the building fabric are basic and have traditional associations. The floors are mainly stone, with some areas of timber or carpet; the walls are stone or plaster; and over the whole spans a laminated timber and boarded roof. Outside, the building is of stone, glass and stainless steel, materials that become part of the earth or part of the sky. Yet the building had to be highly serviced, with air-conditioning to maintain the temperature, humidity and quality of the air, and with sophisticated systems to monitor fire protection and security.

The building is a synthesis of many elements – a Collection of cultural objects spanning four thousand years, a building of components capable of being assembled in five years, and a complex set of devices monitored by computer to preserve the works of art for posterity. The making of this building has been an enthralling experience, not likely to be encountered again. A problem that involves such dimensions of time and craft, and requires the reconciliation of such diverse elements, is unique.

The Hutton Castle Rooms

Ranged around three sides of the Courtyard of the gallery are reconstructions of the Dining Room, Hall and Drawing Room at Hutton Castle, Sir William Burrell's home near Berwick-on-Tweed.

Hutton Castle in the 1950s.

Hutton Castle, spectacularly situated in a commanding position overlooking the river Whitadder, has the colourful history typical of so many Border fortresses, and suffered on several occasions at the hands of English punitive expeditions. When Burrell purchased it in 1916, the house comprised a three-storey keep dating from the 15th or early 16th centuries, to which had been added in the late 16th century a large L-shaped extension. Around the turn of the present century the attractive and picturesque irregularity of the exterior had been "tidied up" by the then owner, Baron Tweedmouth. When Burrell acquired it, he called in his old friend, the distinguished architect Robert Lorimer, to make further alterations, including the addition of an extensive servants' wing and various internal re-arrangements. Unfortunately, Burrell and Lorimer quarrelled irreconcilably over this work, and the former turned to Reginald Fairlie, one of Lorimer's pupils. His efforts too failed to satisfy Burrell. Finally, in the late 1920s the work was completed by Frank Surgey and Wilfred Drake. With their aid and

advice, Hutton Castle was refurbished internally with medieval stone and oak fireplaces and chimneypieces, antique furniture and Eastern carpets, and stained glass, not only in the public rooms but also in the bedrooms. The most important rooms were the Dining Room, Drawing Room and Hall, and it was Burrell's express wish in his Memorandum of Agreement of 1944 that they should be reproduced in the new building to house the Collection.

All three rooms were furnished with velvet curtains, window seats and light shades supplied by leading London firms; these soft furnishings alone cost Burrell £2,000 in the late 1920s and early 1930s, and their quality is attested by their survival in such a good state of preservation. Wooden chandeliers, pelmets and radiator fronts were carved in an early 16th-century style and brass candelabra were supplied to provide a suitable backdrop for the antique contents of the rooms.

The Dining Room

The Dining Room walls are covered by a series of panels carved with linenfold decoration and drolleries, hybrid monsters and foliage, dating from *c.*1500. The armorial achievement over the contemporary stone fireplace is that of the Copledyke family of Harrington Hall in Lincolnshire, almost certainly the original location of the panelling. Displayed on the panelling are three 15th-century tapestry altar frontals. That depicting St Gotthard, Bishop of Hildesheim, and St Pancras bears the arms of the Nuremberg patrician Martin Haller (d.1468) and his wife, Barbara Prunsterin. The largest of the three depicts the Coronation of the Virgin accompanied by five saints, three of whom (Erbanus, Adelarius and Bonifacius) were venerated in Erfurt in Germany, where the tapestry was probably woven. In the heads of the windows are fourteen English shields of arms. The pair in the first window on the left facing into the Courtyard are very early examples of English heraldic glass: they depict the royal arms and the arms of the Clare family and date from the late 13th or early 14th centuries.

The reconstructed Hutton Castle Hall.

The Hutton Castle Dining Room.

The Hutton Castle Dining Room in Burrell's time.

The original Hutton Castle Hall.

In the centre of the room is a large Elizabethan oak refectory table with a parquetry top and carved bulbous legs, and a series of oak armchairs of the late 16th and early 17th centuries are arranged around it. More oak chairs, including a Scottish piece dated 1689, and several oak buffet cupboards and other furniture items of the 16th century are set against the panelling. Placed on this furniture are a number of *objets d'art*, including Late Gothic sculptures and candlesticks. The furnishings of the room are completed by a few items of Oriental and Near Eastern art, the largest being the Persian flower-pattern carpet of 19th-century date, upon which the refectory table is set.

The Hall

The major fittings of the Hall are the stained glass and the stonework. The windows into the Courtyard contain an impressive set of heraldic roundels dating from the latter part of the reign of Henry VIII (c.1537-47) and comprising royal badges and shields of arms. Three of the shields have the arms of Edward VI as Prince of Wales, and one, those of his parents Henry VIII and Jane Seymour, who died in 1537 five days after giving birth to him. There is also some heraldic glass in the south window, but the most important contents of this window are three large German panels depicting, from left to right, Christ appearing to St Mary Magdalen, the Meeting of Joachim and Anne (the parents of the Virgin) at the Golden Gate, and the Adoration of the Magi. They date from the late 15th and early 16th centuries. The principal architectural feature of the room is the stone

fireplace and chimneypiece, a composite of various elements, installed at Hutton Castle in 1937. The original jambs have been replaced by modern stonework. There are some interesting incised graffiti, including the date 1547. On the north wall, the oak doorway into the Tapestry Gallery has in its right spandrel an amusing vignette of a fox, dressed as a bishop, preaching to geese from a pulpit, a

The Adoration of the Magi *stained glass panel in the Hall,* 77.4×57.7cm (30½×22¾in).

Oak "imprisoning" chair in the Hall. English, 16th-century style, height 116.2cm (45¾in).

The Flight into Egypt tapestry in the Hall, 94×77.4cm (37×30½in).

favourite late medieval theme. Built into the west wall is a 14th-century stone canopy and pedestal containing a French painted limestone group of the Virgin and Child, dating from the middle of the 15th century. Amongst the other items of medieval sculpture is a good quality bust of the Virgin, also in limestone and by a French carver. Originally it was probably a full-length figure from an Annunciation group.

The furniture is dominated by the oak refectory table in the centre of the room, which is more than six metres in length and bears the date 1581. The needlework and tapestry coverings of the armchairs and the settee are fine examples of English work of the period c.1650 to 1715; their comfortableness may be contrasted with the oak chair in 16th-century style (probably made for Horace Walpole in the 18th century) which entraps the unwary sitter by means of two iron pinions concealed in the wings. Such "imprisoning chairs" enjoyed a vogue in the 17th century. The diarist Samuel Pepys encountered one in Sir W. Batten's house in 1660: ". . . a chair which he calls King Harry's chaire, where he that sits down is catched with two irons that come round about him which makes great sport."

The most charming of the tapestries in the Hall is the small *Flight into Egypt*, adjacent to the fireplace. This is from a long hanging woven in the first quarter of the 15th century for the Dominican nunnery of Gnadental in Basle, Switzerland, and is based on a version of an early 13th-century poem by Konrad von Heimesfurts on the Assumption of the Virgin. The important French tapestry bearing the arms of William III of Beaufort, his wife Eleanor of Comminges, and their son Raymond, Vicômte de Turenne, is considered in detail in the chapter on tapestries, on page 101. The rugs and carpets are Persian, dating from the 17th to 19th centuries, and the suits of armour are 19th-century reproductions.

The Drawing Room
The Drawing Room is the largest of the suite and was Burrell's main display area at Hutton for tapestries and stained glass. The first window from the left, looking into the Courtyard, contains two 15th-century angels holding shields of arms, which come from the

chapel of the former Hospital of St John at
Northampton, as well as several small English
heraldic panels. A French early 16th-century
Annunciation is distributed over the two main
lights of the centre window, with small
shields of arms and roundels above and
below. The lights at the top contain a medley
of English glass of the 15th century. The chief
elements of the right-hand window are the
full-length figures of St Peter and an
archbishop-saint, both English panels of the
second half of the 15th century. They are
surmounted by two angels of the same period,
painted in East Anglia. At the top is more
English glass, a figure of a female saint and a
late 14th-century bearded donor from a larger
window. The ancient glass in the west
window is confined to the three small lights
and comprises two late 15th-century panels
with the arms of Howard, Duke of Norfolk,
and the Vere Earls of Oxford, separated by a
French roundel depicting the Annunciation
and the cleric who was its donor.

The Drawing Room is of sufficient size to
take some of the bigger tapestries. Between
the windows facing into the Courtyard are
two early 16th-century Franco-Flemish
tapestries from a set of the Labours of the
Months, thought to be a product of the
workshops of Arnoult Poissonnier. The first,
for January, depicts a man seated before a
roaring fire being plied with food and drink
whilst outside a primitive form of golf or
hockey is in progress. The companion
tapestry illustrates the activities associated
with the month of September, with huntsmen
setting ferrets to catch rabbits while in the
background a peasant casts seed on a
ploughed field. Two more Franco-Flemish
hangings in this room belong to the type
known as *millefleurs* because of their
multi-flowered backgrounds. The hanging
Charity Overcoming Envy is described and
illustrated in the chapter on tapestries, page
109; the second one here shows Johannes von
Schleinitz, Bishop of Naumburg (1422-34),
and probably formed part of a series which
was woven in the second quarter of the
16th century, depicting bishops of this See.
Two of the remaining tapestries are from the
Beaufort-Comminges armorial series
described on page 101.

The other textiles in the Drawing Room

consist of Persian and Caucasian rugs and
carpets, and needlework and tapestry
coverings on various chairs and settees.
The rugs and carpets are mainly 19th century.
The furniture coverings are all English,
dating from between *c*.1690 and *c*.1760,
supplemented by several Netherlandish
cushions of the same period. The remaining
furniture is chiefly oak and walnut, dating
from the 17th century. Near the large Late
Gothic stone fireplace and chimneypiece is a
scaled-down version of a longcase clock,
made in the 18th century by the well-known
London firm of Marwick Markham.

Finally, there are some interesting items of
medieval sculpture displayed on tables and in
the two wooden niches on the east wall. Most
are of late 15th or early 16th-century date and
come from the Netherlands or Germany. The
tall group of St Anne holding the Virgin and
the Child Christ, set on the table in front of the
Allegory of Man tapestry on the east wall, is a
notable example of South German limewood
carving. It was one of Burrell's most expensive
purchases of medieval sculpture: he paid £500
for it in 1935.

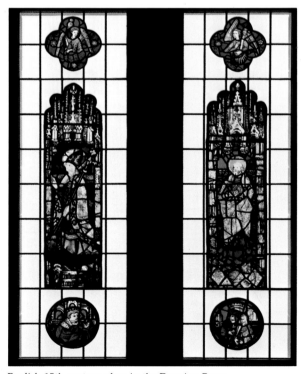

English 15th-century glass in the Drawing Room.

Ancient Civilizations

The majority of the items from the cultures of the ancient world were acquired by Sir William Burrell in the late 1940s and early 1950s, to form the last section of the Collection to be amassed by him. Unlike the antiquities to be found in many other museums, Burrell's were purchased through dealers and not obtained from the distribution of finds from sponsored excavations. In consequence, few of the objects can be allocated to a particular site in their country of origin.

The antiquities come mainly from Egypt, Iraq and Iran, Greece and the eastern Mediterranean, and Italy. Displayed as works of art or craftsmanship, the objects also illustrate historical and cultural developments within their civilizations.

The items from Iraq and Iran, although forming a small part of the Collection as a whole, provide a wide and representative coverage of the material culture of the ancient land of Mesopotamia. This, and their artistic and historical merit, make them one of the main collections in Britain. The earliest periods are reflected in Sumerian alabaster statuettes, stone animal vases and stamp seals. Fragments of reliefs from the palaces of the Assyrian kings are reminders of the might of Ashurbanipal and other rulers mentioned in the Bible. In contrast, the intricate designs of bronze work from Luristan hint at the splendour of the trappings of the nomads of the Iranian highlands.

From Egypt, and forming the largest part of the Ancient Civilizations section, there are some outstanding pieces which illustrate the high degrees of skill reached by this civilization. The earliest work is that of craftsmen in stone, well exemplified by carved vases, bowls and jars of great ornamental

effect. These products of the Predynastic period are followed by relief carvings and sculpture in the round. Characteristic statuettes prepared for private tombs in the New Kingdom may be compared with the monumental relief of the famous king, Rameses II. The block statue of Esmin, from the temple of Amun at Karnak, is contemporary with the beginnings of Greek sculpture. Demonstrating the wide range of objects, there is a rare military badge of polished oyster shell. These and the other choice pieces make the Collection important to the study of ancient Egypt, as comparisons with objects from known sites can be made.

The collection of artefacts from Greece and Italy allows a fairly comprehensive survey of ancient art from those areas to be compiled. The work of the Greek vase painter is well covered, and pride of place should probably go to the bell-*krater* from Lucania in southern Italy. Most striking of the Roman art works is the glorious porphyry head of Zeus or Poseidon, an asset to any collection.

A central feature of the Courtyard in the Burrell Collection is the Warwick Vase. Purchased by the Trustees in 1979, this was an important addition to the Roman antiquities. The original fragments of the 2nd-century A.D. vase, from the ruins of the Emperor Hadrian's villa at Tivoli, were incorporated in a marble reconstruction, possibly by the sculptor Bartolomeo Cavaceppi. Completed about 1775, the cost was borne by Sir William Hamilton, British Envoy to the Court of Naples, who finally presented the vase to his nephew, the 2nd Earl of Warwick. In the late 18th and early 19th centuries it formed a notable source for artists and craftsmen inspired by Neoclassical ideals.

Roman porphyry head of Zeus or Poseidon.

Iraq and Iran

The ancient art of the countries of modern Iraq and Iran is represented in the Collection mainly by objects from Mesopotamia, the classical name for the district between the Tigris and Euphrates rivers. This region became significant in the development of civilization when an efficient method of irrigation was devised which exploited the fertility of the alluvial plain and resulted in agricultural surpluses which could be traded for raw materials otherwise lacking.

The southern part of Mesopotamia, lying between the rivers below the site of modern Baghdad, is most important for tracing the history and culture not only of Iraq but of the ancient Near East in general. The first people who can be distinguished in southern Mesopotamia are the Sumerians. Three distinct and successive Sumerian cultures have been identified through excavation, the earliest being that of Ubaid (c. 4500 B.C.), named after the site where it was first recognized. In this period began the construction of temples with internal niches and mud-brick offering tables. Later, the outer walls of temples were reinforced with buttresses which became a characteristic feature not only in the Predynastic period but also into the Historic period.

The next stage was the Uruk period (c. 3500-3100 B.C.). The name is, again, derived from the site where the temple was an even more imposing building. Among small objects found from sites of this period in southern Mesopotamia and southwest Iran are stone seals used to identify possessions and pendants of animal forms – sheep, ducks and lion heads. An important invention towards the close of the Uruk cultural stage was a system of pictographic writing which was later developed into cuneiform script, so named from the wedge-shaped marks made in wet clay by a stylus (*cuneus* means "wedge" in Latin). The clay, in the shape of oblong tablets, was baked to preserve the form of the signs. At first the signs were written in vertical columns commencing at the top right, but later were turned ninety degrees anticlockwise, to be read horizontally. The

1 *Alabaster statuette, Sumerian, c.2600-2400 B.C., height 36.7cm (14½in).*

IRAQ/IRAN: CHRONOLOGICAL TABLE	
Sumerian	
PREDYNASTIC	
Ubaid	c. 4500-3500 B.C.
Uruk	c. 3500-3100 B.C.
Jemdet-Nasr	c. 3100-2900 B.C.
EARLY DYNASTIC	c. 2900-2370 B.C.
Akkadian	c. 2370-2230 B.C.
Neo-Sumerian	c. 2230-2000 B.C.
Isin-Larsa –	
1st Dynasty of Babylon	c. 2020-1600 B.C.
Kassite	c. 1550-1150 B.C.
Assyrian	
Old	c. 1814-1365 B.C.
Middle	c. 1365-1000 B.C.
Neo	c. 1000-612 B.C.
Neo-Babylonian	626-539 B.C.
Persian (Achaemenid)	539-331 B.C.

tablets record various commodities, such as fish, cattle and barley.

By about 3100 B.C. there was a movement of cultural activity to areas somewhat farther north than Uruk, and in the Jemdet-Nasr period (c. 3100-2900 B.C.) the number of cities grew rapidly. One reason for the decline in the south may have been over-intensive irrigation and an accumulation of salt in the ground. The Collection has an example of a Jemdet-Nasr cylinder seal cut from alabaster whose impression was obtained by rolling the seal over soft clay. At the same time, stamp seals and pendants in simple animal forms continued to be produced.

With the Early Dynastic period (c. 2900-2370 B.C.) Sumerian civilization entered a long, prosperous stage of development with the establishment of a number of city-states. Each city had a patron deity whose temple formed the focal point for administration and organization, the head man of the city being both priest and king.

In southern Mesopotamia, stone suitable for sculpture had to be imported so the products of the workshops were on a small scale. An alabaster standing figure in a pleated skirt, although lacking head and feet, is typical of a votive or "personal" statuette. The angular shape of the chest and elbows was

1 modified in an Early Dynastic statue of c. 2600-2400 B.C. which, apart from the more realistic body, has detailed rendering of the flounced skirt. This figure bears two inscription panels, denoting a person of some status. The purpose of this kind of figure was to act as an effigy of an individual, to be placed in the sanctuary of a religious building to intercede with a deity on the worshipper's **2** behalf. A male head with large eye sockets and carefully executed features is another example from late in the Early Dynastic

2 Alabaster head, Sumerian, c.2600-2400 B.C., height 12cm (4¾in).

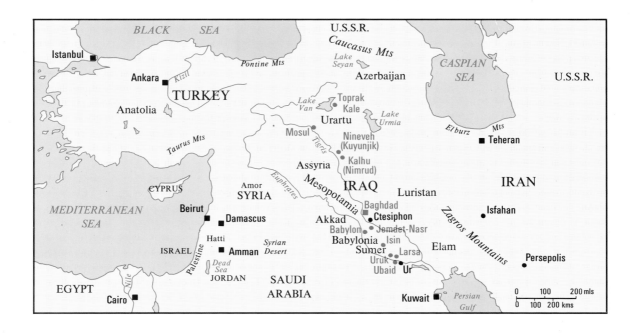

period. Sumerian Dynastic art also features animals figured in relief on vessels and as inlays in stone and shell, represented in the Collection by a bull and cow. These were set in with bitumen, probably as a frieze. Among imported stone was steatite, and an axehead made of this was probably a ritual version of a type which in bronze was used in warfare.

To the north of the Sumerian city-states, a Semitic people had become established in Akkad, a region extending as far as modern Baghdad, and in the Akkadian period (c. 2370-2230 B.C.) political control was exercised over a much larger territory, including Sumer and reaching as far as the Mediterranean. An important consequence of this period was the adoption of Akkadian as the common language of the area, Babylonian and Assyrian being subsequent dialects, written in cuneiform script. Akkadian was later employed as the language for communication between the great powers in the Near East in the 15th and 14th centuries B.C. For example, a file of over 360 cuneiform tablets, written in Akkadian, was recovered from the records office at Tell el Amarna in Egypt. These consisted mainly of diplomatic correspondence between the Egyptian kings Amenophis III and Akhenaten and the rulers of Assyria, Babylonia, Cyprus and Hatti (the kingdom of the Hittites), together with the city kingdoms in Syria and Palestine.

Attackers from the north and west had overwhelmed the Akkadian empire by about 2230 B.C. In the south, however, a new period, the Neo-Sumerian (c. 2230-2000 B.C.), flourished. From this period the Collection possesses a copper figure from a foundation deposit of a temple; he carries on his head a token basket of mortar for use in the building. This Sumerian revival was brought to a close after some two centuries by incursions of Amorites from the west and Elamites from the east.

The beginning of the second millennium (c. 2020-1600 B.C.) saw the reappearance of the city-states, among them Isin and Larsa, followed by the First Dynasty of Babylon. Larsa defeated Isin but was itself crushed by Babylon, whose best-known ruler, Hammurabi, was the author of a famous code of laws. An impressive artefact from the Isin-Larsa period is the almost life-size

3 terra-cotta head of a snarling lion, with looping whiskers and an incised mane. The head was probably intended for incorporation in a temple as a protective figure and still bears traces of its original decoration.

In 1550 B.C. Babylon was sacked by the Hittites, and for the next four centuries Babylonia was ruled by the Kassites who had come from Iran. It was during the Kassite period, coinciding as it did with the Egyptian

3 *Terra-cotta lion head, Isin-Larsa period, height 53.5cm (21in).*

New Kingdom, that diplomatic relations were established between the two powers.

In northern Iraq, based on the area round modern Mosul, Assyria's history began around 1800 B.C. It is divided into three periods, during the last of which, the Neo-Assyrian (c. 1000-612 B.C.), trade, administration, military action and royal leadership all combined to produce a powerful empire. The art of Assyria is best known from the alabaster reliefs of gods and kings and scenes of warfare which decorated the rooms of royal palaces, and of which the Collection has several

4 examples, including the head of a royal attendant from the palace of Ashurnasirpal II (883-859 B.C.) at Nimrud, ancient Kalhu. More than one hundred and fifty years later, the kings Sennacherib and Ashurbanipal had similar decoration in the apartments of their

5 palaces at Nineveh, modern Kuyunjik. Pieces of relief show scribes after a battle recording booty on wax-covered boards, while scenes of warfare are represented by archers,

5 *Stone relief fragment of two scribes, Neo-Assyrian, 704-627 B.C., 18.4×15.2cm (7¼×6in).*

4 *Alabaster relief of an attendant, Assyrian, 9th century B.C., 47×46cm (18½×18½in).*

cavalrymen and camp life, all depicted by the artist in so detailed a manner that a very vivid impression of campaigning conditions is conveyed. Inscriptions on the reliefs and tablets mention events in neighbouring kingdoms, such as Syria to the west, and in the southeast where the Elamites were conquered by Ashurbanipal in *c*.639 B.C.

Another kingdom contemporary with the Assyrians was Urartu, lying to the north between the Caspian and Black Seas, with its capital at Toprak Kale near Lake Van, in

6 modern Turkey. A bull's head in bronze probably comes from this site and was Burrell's last addition to his collection of antiquities. Dating from the late 8th or early 7th century B.C., it would originally have been attached to the rim of a cauldron.

In Luristan, situated in the Zagros mountains of western Iran, nomadic tribes of Cimmerians and Scythians had moved across the Caucasus and settled by *c*.750 B.C. They

were supplied by native smiths with a range of bronze fittings including horse bits,

7 standards, axes, cloak pins and finials, often in the form of stylized animals or a hero between fantastic beasts. Many show the influence of older Mesopotamian motifs. An effective device was the joining of the extremities of pairs of beasts, where slight exaggeration of the horns, ears or snouts was enough to produce a balanced pattern.

The fall of Nineveh in 612 B.C. led to the collapse of the Assyrian empire which was followed by the Neo-Babylonian dynasty, the last native one in Mesopotamia. Babylon in turn fell to the Achaemenid Persians in 539 B.C., who remained until conquest by Alexander the Great in 331 B.C. incorporated the Near East into one vast empire.

6 *Bronze bull's head, Urartian, 7th century B.C., height 14.3cm (5⅝in).*
7 *Bronze finial, Luristan, c.750 B.C., height 7.8cm (3 1/16in).*

Egypt

Situated in the northeast of Africa, with close connections to western Asia, Egypt has certain significant topographical characteristics, the chief of which is the river Nile. Where the Nile flows into the Mediterranean, a delta is formed – broad and flat, interspersed with water channels – while south of Cairo runs the narrow river valley, with only a strip of cultivated land on either side, hemmed in by deserts on both flanks. With little rainfall, life in Egypt always depended on the regular annual rise and flood of the river to provide water and to leave behind a deposit of fertile mud carried by the Blue Nile from the mountains of Ethiopia.

In ancient times, the regular pattern established by the river gave the Egyptians the impression of a balanced permanence, and convinced them that life would continue after death in a manner similar to that enjoyed upon earth. This attitude in turn supplied an impetus to the development of arts and crafts

to a greater extent than in other cultures and explains the need each Egyptian felt to provide, as far as his individual means would allow, certain essentials for his life after death. He required a tomb as the dwelling place for his body, the magical re-creation of life within the tomb by means of carved or painted scenes on the walls, and the provision of model figures and objects to serve him after death. Finally, he needed a statue as a substitute for the body.

A plentiful supply of various types of good-quality stone encouraged a mastery of this long-lasting medium by Egyptian craftsmen. Their products range from small bowls of the hardest stone to enormous structures such as pyramids and temples. The dry conditions which prevail on the desert edge has helped to preserve many of the personal possessions buried with the dead, including organic materials which in less favourable environments would have perished. Thus, a particularly full picture has been built up of ancient Egyptian society, with the archaeological evidence supplemented by a vast body of inscriptions covering religious, magical, mathematical, legal, historical and other subjects.

The earliest evidence of human activity in the Nile Valley is in the form of flint tools from the hills and terraces on the river's edges. About 5000 B.C. stone implements of the Neolithic stage and the introduction of farming appeared in Upper Egypt at Deir Tasa, and at nearby El Badari this type of economy continued with the addition of the first traces of metal – copper beads – and simple tools around 4500 B.C. By about 4000 B.C. two main groups of cultures can be distinguished. The earlier was the Amratian, named after the place where remains were found at El-Amreh in Upper Egypt, and the later Gerzean, from El-Gerzeh in Middle Egypt. In general terms, these formed the early and late phases of the prehistoric, or Predynastic, cultures. They flourished prior to the unification of Egypt in c. 3100 B.C. and the subsequent establishment of a series of dynasties, or ruling families of kings.

The foundations for the later characteristics of Egyptian art were laid in the Predynastic period. In the Amratian phase, burnished red pottery with blackened rims or white-painted linear designs was made; stone vases with lug handles and a small foot were produced, often in basalt; and a range of flint implements was available, including the "fishtail" lance-head. The Gerzean culture, on the evidence from

cemeteries, shows a different type of pottery from that of the south, with jars made of buff-coloured pottery decorated with reddish paint. During this phase the manufacture of stone vases was further developed by the use of materials such as marble, breccia and other hard stones. Slate was also used, as in a cosmetic palette, the personal possession of a Predynastic Egyptian and the kind of item often buried with the deceased owner.

Unification in c.3100 B.C. brought together the kingdoms of Upper and Lower Egypt, which had been formed in the later Predynastic period from previous confederations of districts in the south and north. This dual concept of the Two Kingdoms was to remain all through the Historic period of Egypt.

At the beginning of the Historic period, the 1st and 2nd Dynasties, known as the Archaic period, witnessed the establishment of a central administration based on the capital at Memphis at the apex of the Nile delta and saw the introduction of a system of writing – hieroglyphic script. Also in this period, the artistic conventions, craft methods and life style of the Egyptians rapidly progressed to the forms which they were to retain, with only slight alterations, for centuries to come.

A good indication of the skill and resource of the Egyptians of the Archaic period is given by the mastery with which they fashioned stone bowls of fine quality. In addition to smaller items, such as the calcite jar, or

1 furniture, like the alabaster offering table, the technique of the mason was, in the succeeding Old Kingdom of the 3rd to 6th Dynasties (c.2780-2250 B.C.), applied also to architecture. The masonry could be decorated

2 with scenes carved in relief and enhanced with paint, particularly on the interior walls of tomb chapels, to give a vivid impression of

EGYPT: CHRONOLOGICAL TABLE

Dates are approximate with the margin of error decreasing as more recent times are reached.

Prehistoric

PREDYNASTIC

Tasian/Badarian	before 4000 B.C.
Amratian	4000-3500 B.C.
Gerzean	3500-3100 B.C.

Historic

ARCHAIC PERIOD

1st Dynasty	3100-2980 B.C.
2nd Dynasty	2980-2780 B.C.

OLD KINGDOM

3rd Dynasty	2780-2680 B.C.
4th Dynasty	2680-2565 B.C.
5th Dynasty	2565-2420 B.C.
6th Dynasty	2420-2250 B.C.

FIRST INTERMEDIATE PERIOD

7th-10th Dynasties	2250-2050 B.C.

MIDDLE KINGDOM

11th Dynasty	2134-1991 B.C.
12th Dynasty	1991-1786 B.C.

SECOND INTERMEDIATE PERIOD

13th-17th Dynasties	1786-1560 B.C.

NEW KINGDOM

18th Dynasty	1560-1304 B.C.
19th Dynasty	1304-1200 B.C.
20th Dynasty	1200-1085 B.C.

LATE PERIOD

THIRD INTERMEDIATE PERIOD

21st Dynasty	1085-945 B.C.
22nd Dynasty	945-715 B.C.
23rd Dynasty	818-720 B.C.
24th Dynasty	730-715 B.C.
25th Dynasty	747-656 B.C.
26th Dynasty	664-525 B.C.
27th Dynasty	525-404 B.C.
28th Dynasty	404-398 B.C.
29th Dynasty	398-378 B.C.
30th Dynasty	378-341 B.C.
31st Dynasty	341-332 B.C.

PTOLEMAIC PERIOD	332-30 B.C.

1 *Stone jar and table, Old Kingdom, height of jar 12.7cm (5in).*

daily life. This tradition was continued, with variations in later times, to culminate in the monumental figures and scenes carved on temples, and in the appearance of sculpture in the round.

2 *Limestone relief of an offering bearer, 6th Dynasty, 31.7×39.3cm (12½×15½in).*

3 *Limestone head from a pair statuette, 18th Dynasty, height 21.5cm (8½in).*
4 *Wooden shawabti of Hori-Nakhte, 19th Dynasty, height 24.1cm (9½in).*

After a breakdown of central control in the First Intermediate period, the country was reunited in the flourishing age called the Middle Kingdom – the 11th and 12th Dynasties (*c.*2050-1786 B.C.). From this time come pots of nonporous stone, and the exploitation in statuettes of the durable qualities of stones like basalt. There followed another decline into internal confusion – the Second Intermediate period – compounded by the infiltration from western Asia of the Hyksos people, after which Egypt once more gained independent unity under the princes of Thebes. They inaugurated the New Kingdom of the 18th to 20th Dynasties (*c.*1560-1085 B.C.) when Egypt became an imperial power and reached her peak.

In these settled and prosperous conditions, there was an increase in the amount of raw materials and products from petty kingdoms which owed allegiance to Egypt. A growing body of highly trained craftsmen was able to satisfy a widening demand for quality articles and even luxuries. More private individuals

3 were able to commission statues on which details of costume and headdress were depicted. Stone continued to be used for household items, such as handled jugs for tableware. Royal and temple workshops employed sculptors to carve appropriate

6 figures of the gods, for example Sekhmet, the lioness-headed goddess. Soldiers, leaders of campaigns in Asia and Nubia, were depicted in statues bearing their military titles, like that of Pa-ra-her-wenem-if, the third son of

5 *Granite relief of Rameses II, height 59cm (23¼in).*

6 *Granite head of Sekhmet, 18th Dynasty, height 30.4cm (12in).*

8 *Basalt head of a queen, Late period, height 15.8cm (6¼in).*
9 *Glass amphora, Late period, height 6.6cm (2⅝in).*

Rameses II, King of Egypt (*c.*1290-24 B.C.). Rameses' reign saw war with the Hittites and the construction of many colossal monuments, including the rock temple of
5 Abu Simbel. A relief showing his head is in the Collection.

    Individuals had stelae set up in their tombs, on which family relationships were often depicted, together with requests for continuing offerings of provisions for the hereafter. *Shawabti* figures were included in
4 burials to act as substitutes for the deceased if they were called on to serve in work gangs in the next world. By the end of the New Kingdom, mummification of the body was being perfected. The process entailed the removal for separate embalmment of the internal organs, which were placed in Canopic jars.

    By the close of the 20th Dynasty (*c.*1085 B.C.) the great days of Egypt as a world power were past. The ensuing Late Period (*c.*1085-332 B.C.) included the Third Intermediate period with the country again divided. Then, from the south, an invasion by Nubian kings to form the 25th Dynasty (*c.*750-656 B.C.) restored unity, but a native revival by the 26th Dynasty of Sais in the delta drove the Nubians out. This period witnessed

7 *Bronze statuette of Osiris. Late Period, height 48.2cm (19in).*

many splendid pieces of craftsmanship,
8 particularly statues in stone, as in the head of a queen, and in bronze, as exemplified by the
7 fine figure of Osiris, god of the underworld. Delicate vessels in glass, such as the little
9 perfume bottle, illustrate yet another craft, first established during the 18th Dynasty.

    The conquest of Egypt by Alexander the Great in 332 B.C. brought in the Greek rule of the Ptolemaic period (332-30 B.C.). The influence of the Greek world made itself felt, but the old religious beliefs and funerary practices continued, including the use of huge
10 stone outer coffins, a head from one of which is illustrated.

10 *Syenite head from a coffin lid, Ptolemaic period, height 36.8cm (14½in).*

Greece

The early development of material culture in Greece can be traced through the evidence left behind by the wandering hunters and food-gatherers of the Early and Middle Stone Ages. The earliest settlement began about 6000 B.C. when a Neolithic technology was practised to produce pottery, a range of stone and obsidian tools, and weapons such as axes, blades and arrow heads, with bone being used for awls, pins and polishers.

In the succeeding Bronze Age, introduced from the older civilizations of the east, developments in the Aegean area can be followed in three main centres: the mainland of Greece, the island of Crete and the island chain of the Cyclades. From about 3000 B.C. and for the next thousand years, each region experienced almost parallel and continuous technological advance. In effect, it was a transition from an economy dependent on stone and bone to one where metal gradually became established without ousting the former materials entirely.

The arrival in Crete about 3000 B.C. of immigrants from Asia Minor was the beginning of the Minoan civilization which absorbed the indigenous Neolithic population. Their settlements consisted of a number of small communities in the centre and east of the island where, under peaceful conditions, the skills of craftsmen using improved working methods, for example, drills and bits with abrasives to grind out

stone vases, showed steady progress. A stone palette in the Collection illustrates just such skills. After 2000 B.C. there were changes. In Crete the Bronze Age was in full swing, culminating in the Middle Minoan palaces of Knossos, Phaistos and others. These great buildings were planned, provided with elaborate drainage systems and had their plastered walls decorated with frescoes, while their owners, the Minoan sea-kings, extended their realm over the Aegean.

It was otherwise on the Greek mainland where an invasion by the first Greek-speaking peoples occurred about 1900 B.C. In this instance we can look in vain for a well-established civilization comparable to that of the Minoans. It is possible, however, that increased contacts with the Cretans about 1500 B.C. had an influence on developments on the mainland where the Mycenaean civilization, named after Mycenae, its chief centre, emerged. By the middle of the 15th century B.C. Mycenae had extended its empire and controlled the neighbouring islands, including Crete itself. Outstanding among the monuments of the city of Mycenae were its fortifications, particularly the Lion Gate set in its walls, and its enormous stone-lined tombs. The pottery of the period was characterized by
1 painted styles, such as the stem cup decorated with simple designs. Terra-cotta figurines had a wide distribution and continued to be produced into the 12th century B.C. Another aspect of the Mycenaeans is shown in a

CHRONOLOGY OF GREEK ART STYLES	
Minoan	*c.* 3000-1500 B.C.
Mycenaean	*c.* 1400-1100 B.C.
Protogeometric	*c.* 1025-900 B.C.
Geometric	*c.* 900-700 B.C.
Archaic	*c.* 700-480 B.C.
Orientalizing style	700-600 B.C.
Corinthian	625-550 B.C.
Classic	*c.* 500-325 B.C.
Hellenistic	*c.* 325-100 B.C.

1 *Earthenware stem cup, Mycenaean, c.1200 B.C., height 18.4cm (7¼in).*

2 model chariot with riders which probably accompanied a burial of about 1250 B.C. This object was found on Cyprus, a fact which illustrates the trading links which had been established across the eastern Mediterranean.

2 *Earthenware model chariot, Mycenaean-Cypriot, c.1250 B.C., height 9.8cm (3⅞in).*
3 *Earthenware perfume vase, Rhodian, 6th century B.C., height 5.7cm (2¼in).*

Following the collapse of Mycenae about 1025 B.C., a dark age occurred in Greece when artistic activity was represented mainly by painted pottery. In the Protogeometric style (c.1025-900 B.C.) simple designs of circles and wavy lines were introduced, while patterns using straight lines, later supplemented by human and animal figures, were featured in the Geometric style (c.900-700 B.C.). Again, such wares have been found in the islands of the eastern Mediterranean as well as Greece; for example, from Cyprus comes an amphora and, perhaps reflecting the previous warlike Mycenaean influence, a mounted warrior. To the 8th century B.C. belong small statuettes, such as a bronze horse cast in one piece. Each of these statuettes was unique as the mould in which it was made had to be broken up and discarded to release the casting. The horse shows fairly elementary modelling methods and an unsophisticated concept of the animal's structure.

With the Archaic period (c.700-480 B.C.) Greece gradually emerged from its dark age. The geometric patterns on vases were steadily replaced by scenes incorporating figures, and, as a result of greatly expanded trade, influences and motifs from the Near East formed the basis of the Orientalizing style (c.700-600 B.C.). By the middle of the 7th century B.C., Corinth, one of the most expansionist of the city-states which had

evolved since the fall of Mycenae, had come to prominence in the manufacture of pottery. On a Corinthian *aryballos,* or scent bottle, the decoration shows the figures of sirens with a lotus, palmette and rosettes, all of eastern origin.

As the populations increased, Greeks from the mainland city-states began to colonize southern Italy, Sicily and western Asia Minor, as well as the Dodecanese islands of the eastern Aegean. Settlements were founded which were independent but retained strong religious, linguistic and cultural ties with the Greek mainland while developing their own styles. On the island of Rhodes, perfume vases were made in moulds, one shape **3** imitating the helmeted head of a warrior. The Greek colonists, traders and mercenaries also received ideas and techniques for painting and for sculpture from Egypt, now in the 26th Saite Dynasty (c.664-525 B.C.) and enjoying an artistic revival.

Athens in the middle of the 6th century B.C. ousted Corinth as the principal pottery producer in Greece. To begin with, Attic vases used the same black-figure method as the

4 *Earthenware black-figure amphora and lekythos, Attic Greek, late 6th-early 5th century B.C., height of amphora 40cm (15¾in).*

Corinthians, in which the decoration was painted in black silhouette on the pot with some white and red applied. The broad swelling body of the amphora provided a particularly suitable surface for painters, and one in the Collection, dated to *c.*540 B.C., illustrates the technique well. Its design features a common motif of warriors preparing for battle, putting on their accoutrements, departing for a campaign, or engaged in combat. Here, a young soldier is fitting greaves on to his legs, his crested helmet on the ground beside him; in front of him a woman stands holding his spear and shield while two comrades in arms, ready to march off, watch the young man's preparations. The design on the *kylix,* or drinking cup, bears a gorgon head inside while on the outside a sphinx appears between large eyes.

About 530 B.C. the technique of red-figure vase painting was introduced, in which the body of the pot was coloured black and the figures in the decoration left in the reddish colour of the vase itself. Although black-figured vases were made for many more years, the new method was increasingly adopted as it allowed the painter to render the human body more realistically.

Towards the close of the Archaic period the Greek states, first in Asia Minor and later on the mainland, were attacked by the Persians. The invasion was beaten back, and in the following Classic period (*c.*500-325 B.C.) Greece reached the highest point of its achievements in architecture, literature, science and art. The Classical style can be seen in vase painting: a *pyxis,* or toilet box with lid, depicts a scene of women and *erotes* (winged gods of love) with a panther; while, belonging to the same period of the early 5th century B.C., a *lekythos,* or oil jug, reflects in its decoration another aspect of Greek life, with a seated musician playing a stringed instrument to an audience.

The Persian invasion of the opening years of the Classic period and then internal strife between Athens and Sparta in the Peloponnesian War (431-404 B.C.) did much to develop the craft of the armourer. Sheets of bronze were hammered and shaped to form close-fitting helmets with protective nose pieces. How much bronze sculpture that was

5 *Earthenware black-figure* kylix, *Attic Greek, 6th century* B.C., *diameter 22.2cm (8¾in).*

6 *Bronze helmet, Corinthian, 6th century* B.C., *height 22.2cm (8¾in).*

7 *Gold mirror cover, Greek, 4th century* B.C., *diameter 13.9cm (5½in).*
8 *Gold earrings, Greek, 5th century* B.C., *height 2.5cm (1in).*

9 *Bronze bust of Hermes, Roman copy, 1st century* B.C.-*1st century* A.D., *of Greek original, height 41.9cm (16½in).*

in existence but was broken up and re-cast as armour can be judged from later copies. One of these is a Roman copy of an original Greek 5th-century B.C. bust of Hermes, the messenger of the gods.

Stone sculpture also progressed in the Classic period, and remains of statuary include the marble head of a woman or goddess belonging to the 4th century B.C. To the same period can be assigned a seated terra-cotta statue representing Cybele, the goddess of nature worshipped in Phrygia and later adopted throughout Greece. Dressed in an ankle-length tunic, or chiton, Cybele is shown on a high-backed seat with her feet resting on a footstool.

Following the conquests of Alexander the Great of Macedon, the Greek world entered the Hellenistic period (325-100 B.C.). An increase in the supply of gold, obtained as booty from conquered eastern states, encouraged the goldsmith's art. Examples in the Collection include the finely worked cover for a mirror case and a pair of earrings which feature a bull's head in their design. A silver ladle of the 3rd or 2nd centuries B.C., probably from Asia Minor, shows that precious metals could be used for functional articles. As with the statuary of the Classic period, generally only known from later Roman copies, so a marble torso of Aphrodite, the Greek goddess of love, made in the 2nd century A.D., is based on a Hellenistic statue.

Italy

The Greeks who colonized southern Italy and Sicily in the 8th and 7th centuries B.C. established their settlements to the south of the area of Etruria. The Etruscan civilization, which appears to have evolved from the Early Iron Age culture known as Villanovan, was affected considerably by the presence of the Greek colonists and Phoenician merchants who were interested in the exploitation of Etruria's metal-bearing ores.

Owing to the availability of suitable ores for bronze, Etruscan craftsmanship in this area was of a high standard, particularly in the Archaic period (c. 600-470 B.C.). The bronzesmith produced arms and armour, including helmets, as well as household equipment in the form of characteristic beaked jugs of the early 5th century B.C. Bronze statuettes, for example, warriors in armour, were placed as offerings in shrines.

Pottery typical of Etruscan style was termed *bucchero* ware. The dark-grey fabric of the pots was obtained by firing the clay in a kiln from which oxygen was excluded. A common shape was the *kantharos,* or two-handled drinking cup, which had its counterpart in Greek vessels.

In the southern part of Italy, the influence of Greece is evident in the Corinthian-style pottery of the 6th century B.C. From this period a typical *olpe,* or jug, is in the Collection. South Italian red-figure vase painting began in the 5th century B.C. with types similar to those made in Athens. The Peloponnesian War disrupted the supply of pottery from Greece and forced local potters to meet the demand. From Lucania, an 1 excellent specimen of a bell-*krater,* a bowl for mixing wine, has survived. It is by the Sydney Painter, so named after a vase with similar decoration, now in the Nicholson Museum of Sydney University in Australia, and dates from 360-340 B.C. Another school of potters operated in Apulia, and from this region the Collection possesses other red-figure vessels, among them a column-*krater,* also for wine; an *askos,* or lamp filler, in the form of a duck; and 1 a rhyton, or drinking cup, made in a mould in

1 *Earthenware bell-*krater *and sheep's-head rhyton, South Italian, 4th century* B.C., *height of bell-*krater *22.7cm (9in).*

2 *Porphyry head of Zeus or Poseidon, Roman,* c.A.D. 320-330, *after a Greek bronze, height 34.5cm (13⅜in).*

3 *Mosaic of a cockerel, Roman, 1st century* B.C., *35.5×30cm (14×11⅞in).*

the shape of a sheep's head. Each of these Apulian pieces belongs to the 4th century B.C.

From farther south, from the late 4th-century tombs at Centuripae in Sicily, there are two earthenware heads in the Collection. They represent Demeter, the goddess of agriculture, and her daughter Persephone who symbolized the renewed growth each year of all vegetation.

The region of Latium, where later Rome emerged as the main city, was, from the point of view of craftsmanship, overshadowed by its neighbour Etruria until the mid-4th century B.C. During this period, however, bronzesmithing was developing, particularly at Praeneste, where a *cista,* or toilet box, engraved with a design of warriors in combat, was produced.

The examples of Roman Art on display cover a range of materials. In stone sculpture,

2 the porphyry head of Zeus or Poseidon is a Roman copy of *c.* A.D. 320-330 of a 5th-century B.C. Greek bronze. The headless marble statue of a boy is of the 1st century A.D.

3 A fine mosaic, featuring a cockerel, indicates the style of decoration to be found in a house or public building. The tiny size of the individual tesserae, the cubes of stone used to build up the image of the bird's plumage, may be noted. Many domestic fittings and utensils were made from bronze. For cooking, a *patera,* or saucepan, was used not only in the kitchen but also by soldiers as a mess tin. A heavy bronze female figure may be part of a hearth fitting, while a silver spoon of the 3rd or 4th centuries A.D. could have been for daily use or for display as a rare item, to indicate the owner's standing in society.

CHRONOLOGY OF ITALIAN CULTURE STAGES	
Iron Age (Villanovan Culture)	*c.* 900-720 B.C.
Orientalizing period	*c.* 720-600 B.C.
Archaic period	*c.* 600-470 B.C.
Classic period	*c.* 470-320 B.C.
Hellenistic period	*c.* 320-100 B.C.
Roman Republican	*c.* 500-27 B.C.
Imperial	27 B.C.-*c.* A.D. 425

Oriental Art

Although approximately one quarter of his Collection comprises Oriental material, the source of Sir William Burrell's interest in the arts of the East remains a mystery. There is nothing to indicate from whence that interest sprang, and we can only assume that he saw examples, perhaps in the homes of friends or possibly in museums, and was attracted by them.

Very little is known about the Oriental items he bought before 1911, but from his purchase books dating from 1911 to 1957 we know that throughout that time he collected Chinese ceramics almost every year, with his most prolific buying period in this field being in the 1940s – from 1945 to 1948 he bought more than 120 pieces a year. Some of his finest purchases were made during this period, including the magnificent figure of a *lohan*, illustrated here.

Sir William expressed in his letters not only his fondness for early Chinese ceramics but also for Chinese bronzes and his particular appreciation of their patina. He seems to have bought them fairly steadily throughout the years of the purchase books, and, as with the ceramics, showed a distinct preference for fine works of the early periods.

The jades he seems to have purchased mainly during the 1940s. The Collection includes some rather elegant vessels, early weapons and ritual objects, plaques and pendants and a delightful selection of small animal figures.

The Near Eastern carpets Sir William appears to have bought fairly consistently from his early collecting days but ceased to purchase after 1940. He obviously derived considerable pleasure from them as they were in many rooms of his home at Hutton Castle.

Most of the Near Eastern pottery and the few items of metalwork were bought after 1946, and indeed the majority of the Turkish Iznik wares were purchased in 1947. These latter obviously had considerable appeal for him, as did the lustrewares of Persia. Most of

the Near Eastern ceramic wares and carpets in the Collection are the products of Islamic communities. The Muslim era starts in the Christian year A.D. 622, that being the year when the Prophet Mohammed, the founder of the Islamic faith, migrated from Mecca to Medina. This migration is called the Hegira. The Muslim era is reckoned in lunar years from that date, and the years are prefixed by A.H., standing for Anno Hegirae.

Under the Prophet Mohammed's successors, the Muslim armies expanded their sphere of influence from the Arabian peninsula, and by the middle of the 7th century A.D. controlled an enormous area spreading across Egypt, Syria, Iraq and Persia. Anatolia, modern Turkey, was brought under Muslim influence after A.D. 1071. Despite the devastation caused by the Mongol invasions of the early 13th century, by the end of the century Islam was established as the official religion of the Il-Khanid Dynasty in Persia. Other dynasties ruled the other parts of the Near East in a complex and frequently changing pattern, but the area was united in its adherence to the Islamic faith.

For the Chinese material it has been possible to produce a chronology which is largely self-explanatory except for a few periods. The period of the Warring States (403-221 B.C.), for instance, was an era when although China was nominally ruled by the Zhou kings, in practice the power was in the hands of the individual states who contended with each other for supremacy. The periods that fall between the end of the Han Dynasty in A.D. 220 and the beginning of the Sui Dynasty in A.D. 581 are a complex succession of divisions of power within changing geographical areas. The Liao and Jin Dynasties were both "foreign" dynasties which controlled parts of northern China during the native Song Dynasty.

Chinese polychrome lohan *figure.*

Chinese Ceramics

The Burrell Collection is fortunate in possessing fine examples of most of the main types of pottery and porcelain produced in China during her long ceramic history. From the Neolithic period to the present day – a span of over 5,000 years – the Chinese potter has frequently been the initiator of sophisticated techniques; on occasion the perfector of ideas gleaned from elsewhere; and, outstandingly, an artist who married decorative motif to vessel shape with consummate skill.

The earliest Chinese ceramics in the Collection are painted pots associated with the Neolithic Yangshao culture which was centred on Gansu province in the northwest but also spread eastwards into Shaanxi and Henan. Pottery-making was obviously an important and established activity in China even at this early date, as has been shown by archaeological excavations in the People's Republic of China. The village site of Banpo in Shaanxi province, for example, was divided into three separate areas: for habitation, for burial and for pottery-making. Archaeological excavations have also enabled us to identify certain decorative schemes with certain areas. It is possible, for instance, to say

1 *Neolithic painted urn, Yangshao culture, 3rd millenium* B.C., *height 30.4cm (12in).*

1 that the urn here is of the type found at Machang in Gansu province and can be dated to the 3rd millenium B.C. Pots of this sort from Machang and various other sites are earthenware and were made by the coiling method. This particular urn shape, with constricted neck and bulbous body narrowing to a small base, is the one most frequently found among excavated material. It is remarkably light in weight for its size, and can be decorated in variations of red, black, brown and a purplish colour. The decoration characteristically covers only the top half of the urn, and in the case of the Burrell pieces derives its motifs from a geometric repertoire, although animal, fish, and very occasionally human motifs are known from other sites.

In the succeeding Bronze Age, at least in the early periods, the ceramics were predictably overshadowed by the bronzes, of which the Collection has a fine selection. The only major developments in pottery were the introduction during the Shang Dynasty (c.1600-1027 B.C.) of a heavy white earthenware with carved decoration deriving from contemporary bronze designs; the introduction of incised and carved decoration to add to the impressed, scratched or pricked surfaces of the earlier wares; and the introduction of deliberate glazing.

It is probable that the first glazing effect on ceramics was achieved accidentally when ash containing silica fell on vessels whilst they were being fired in a kiln. This effect is known as kiln glost, and it is found occasionally even on ceramics of very early periods. The first examples of vessels to which glaze was applied before they were placed in the kiln appear in China during the Shang Dynasty – probably sometime between 1300 and 1027 B.C. The technique was developed during the Zhou period, and by the Han Dynasty (206 B.C.-A.D. 220) glazed wares were firmly established.

Some of the most impressive of the Han glazed wares are the high-fired earthenwares with greenish-brown glazes, which were made in the east of China, possibly in northern Zhejiang province. A fine example

2 *Lidded jar, Han Dynasty, 1st century B.C.-1st century A.D., height 35.5cm (14in).*

mythological figures among the peaks. The origin of the shape of these jars, which are sometimes made as incense burners and are also found in bronze is obscure, but it is probably a combination of the Five Sacred Mountains of China and the island home of the Daoist immortals in the Eastern Sea.

Elaborate burials necessitating the interment of a large number of items with the deceased go back to Shang times when, for the funerals of members of the aristocracy and high-ranking officials, not only all kinds of precious objects but also servants, slaves and animals were buried with their masters to serve them in the next world. During the succeeding Zhou period this gruesome practice declined, and wooden or straw figures tended to be substituted. By the Han Dynasty, beautiful ceramic models were being made, not only of people and animals like the

3 rather endearing watchdog with his carefully detailed harness, dating from the 1st century B.C. or the 1st century A.D., but also mundane items such as stoves, well-heads and carts, of which the Collection also has excellent examples. On a larger scale, ceramic buildings of various kinds were also produced. One of

4 the most impressive is the storehouse in three sections which stands almost a metre high. This is interesting not only as a supreme example of the early ceramic craftsman's skill but also for the wealth of information it

2 of this type is a large lidded jar with the characteristic three bands of decoration on the shoulder. Between the raised lines birds are incised into the body of the jar and highlighted by the ash, or feldspathic, glaze. The two handles surmounted by their bovine masks are in a style similar to those on contemporary bronze vessels.

It was also during the Han Dynasty that lead glazes first appeared in China. These lead-fluxed glazes can be fired only at a low temperature and so during this period are found exclusively on low-fired earthenwares. The most popular colours were various brown and green shades, but since the lead glazes are very soft they have often degraded during burial to produce a rather attractive silvery iridescence. They are also poisonous so their use was mainly confined to items made specifically for burial with the dead. Among these mortuary wares are many which employed a technique which had only recently been applied to ceramics: that of moulding. Moulding was used to decorate an even surface – such as that of a cylinder – and also to produce a more dramatically three-dimensional shape, as can be seen very

3 well on the *Boshanlu*, or hill jar. These jars are characteristic of the Han Dynasty, and depict animals and figures in a landscape around the base, while the lid is made in the shape of a hill or mountain with animals, hunters and

3 *Watchdog and* Boshanlu *jar and cover, Han Dynasty, height of jar 23.4cm (9⅛in), height of dog 38.1cm (15in).*

4 *Model of storehouse, Han Dynasty, 206 B.C.-220 A.D., height 95.2cm (37½in).*

provides about early Chinese architecture. It shows clearly details of the roof construction, the complex bracketing system under the eaves, the patterned screens, and various other aspects of architectural style that were to remain integral parts of Chinese buildings for many centuries.

Ceramic burial objects reached a peak of magnificence during the Tang Dynasty (A.D. 618-907), particularly in the first half of the 8th century before the An Lushan rebellion of A.D. 756. This was an attempt by a regional commander to overthrow the dynasty, which in fact managed to survive for another century and a half, but without its former splendour and influence. The sophisticated members of the Tang ruling classes were less inclined to concern themselves with prosaic items like cooking stoves, and so most of the funerary wares depict figures of elegantly dressed persons and elaborately caparisoned animals. Indeed, probably the best known of the Tang Dynasty models are the horses and camels, both of which are represented by fine examples in the Collection. The very

5 handsome horse is, like the Han pieces, made of lead-glazed earthenware but with more than one glaze colour. This *sancai,* or three-colour, ware flourished during the first half of the 8th century and is found on vessels as well as figures. The name is slightly misleading since more than three colours are sometimes used, but the basic palette was green, amber and cream, with occasional additions of black or cobalt blue. The horse is also interesting for his trappings which reflect Persian Sassanian influence, while the cosmopolitanism of the Tang court at Changan (modern Xi'an) is further

5 emphasized by the costume of the attendant who stands beside him wearing Central Asian dress. It is typical of the human or semi-human figures that, as on this figure, the face and neck are left unglazed and are painted with unfired pigments. Whole figures were also decorated in this way – a technique developed during the Han Dynasty – but the pigments did not survive burial very well. Cream-glazed figures were also made, particularly in the 7th century, and these too were often decorated with unfired pigments.

As well as human figures, models were made of members of the spirit world to stand

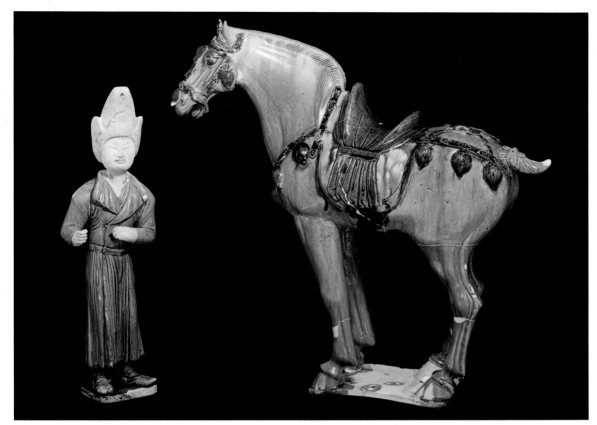

5 *Polychrome horse and attendant figure, Tang Dynasty, 8th century* A.D.*, height of horse 50.8cm (20in) attendant 41.9cm (16½in).*

guard against evil spirits in Tang Dynasty tombs. These were either *qitou* figures in grotesque animal shape, or *fangxiang* figures in exaggerated human form, like those which stand at the northern entrance to the Collection's Oriental Daylit Gallery.

The Tang potter did not, however, restrict himself to producing tomb figures. The *sancai* glaze was also used to great effect on pots. In addition, various other decorative techniques were adopted. The elaborate medallions on the elegant cream-glazed ewer, for example, were moulded separately and then attached to the body of the vessel – like the tassels on the *sancai* horse's harness – while the dragon's-head handle has been freely modelled. As well as earthenwares with lead glazes, stoneware vessels with alkaline or feldspathic glazes were also produced during the Tang Dynasty, some of the most attractive being those with dark-brown or black opaque glazes suffused with bluish-grey, such as the jar with its characteristic domed lid which dates from the 8th or 9th centuries A.D.

Two further very important wares were established during this period. One of these was the white porcelain ware developed in northern China, that was to have such a

tremendous impact not only on the ceramic art of China but also on that of the Near East. The other was fine-quality *yue* ware made in northern Zhejiang province: a stoneware with a fine-grained, dense, pale-grey body covered by a green transparent glaze which could be more bluish or yellowish depending on the reduction or oxidization in the firing. This

6 *Ewer with dragon's-head handle and jar with lid, Tang Dynasty, 8th-9th century* A.D.*, height of ewer 36.8cm (14½in).*

CHINESE CHRONOLOGY

Neolithic	c.7th millenium-c.1600 B.C.
Shang Dynasty	c.1600-c.1027 B.C.
Western Zhou Dynasty	c.1027-771 B.C.
Eastern Zhou Dynasty	771-256 B.C.
Spring and Autumn Annals period	722-481 B.C.
Warring States period	403-221 B.C.
Qin Dynasty	221-206 B.C.
Han Dynasty	206 B.C.-A.D. 220
Western Han Dynasty	206 B.C.-A.D. 8
Interregnum	A.D. 8-23
Eastern Han Dynasty	A.D. 25-220
Three Kingdoms and Western Jin	219-316
Eastern Jin and Five Principalities	317-419
Nanbeichao I	420-500
Nanbeichao II	501-580
Sui Dynasty	581-618
Tang Dynasty	618-907
Five Dynasties	907-960
Liao Dynasty (northeast China)	947-1125
Song Dynasty	960-1279
Northern Song Dynasty	960-1126
Southern Song Dynasty	1127-1279
Jin Dynasty (north China)	1115-1234
Yuan Dynasty	1260-1368
Ming Dynasty	1368-1644
Qing Dynasty	1644-1912
Republic	1912-1949
People's Republic	1949-

8 Yue *ware vase, 10th century* A.D., *height 33.6cm (13¼in).*
7 *Polychrome* fangxiang *tomb guardian figures. Tang
Dynasty, 8th century* A.D., *height 93.9cm (36in).*

type of ware had been produced in the area
before the Tang Dynasty but had not been of
such superb quality as that made between the
late 8th and the 10th centuries. One of the
shapes characteristic of the *yue* wares of the
8 10th century is the long-necked vase with
petals incised around the body. This example
also has a very attractive leaf-shaped lid with a
fan-tailed bird finial.

The tradition of green-glazed stoneware
was carried on in the ceramics known as
northern celadons which were made
primarily at the kilns around Yaozhou in
Shaanxi province or Linru Xian in Henan
province. The ware originated in the 9th
century, but it was not until the 10th century
that it was fully established, reaching its
peak during the Northern Song Dynasty
(A.D. 960-1126). The body is once again grey
stoneware, and it is covered by a transparent
soft green glaze. The glaze colour is produced
by a fairly small amount of iron oxide which
changes from ferric oxide to ferrous oxide
when it is fired in a reducing atmosphere –
that is, one deprived of oxygen. The tone of
the colour depends on how this reducing
atmosphere is controlled. The rather elegantly
9 shaped bowl has been left undecorated except
for the bands around the rim, but other
examples have either carved or moulded
decoration under the glaze.

From the Northern Song Dynasty onwards,
these celadon wares were much admired in
China and have been produced in various
forms up to the present day. The name
"celadon" itself is of European origin, from a
pastoral romance of 1610 by Honoré D'Urfé,
called *L'Astrée*. The shepherd in the play was
called Celadon and wore a costume trimmed
with grey-green ribbons – hence the name.

When the Song court was forced by the
invading Tartars to flee from Kaifeng in 1127
and set up its capital at Hangzhou in Zhejiang
province, the southern kilns were favoured by
royal patronage and expanded accordingly.
One of the southern wares to find royal favour
was another celadon ware, known as *longquan*
celadon after the name of the main town of the
area in Zhejiang and northern Fujian province
where the kilns were situated. This southern
celadon differs in a number of ways from its
northern counterpart. The body varies from a
dense grey stoneware to an almost white

porcellanous ware, and on all except the whitest pieces where it is exposed in the kiln it fires to a reddish brown. Unlike the northern ware, the *longquan* celadons have a slightly opaque glaze, caused by tiny bubbles in the glaze and also by the presence of plant ash.

9 The small bowl with carved petals on the outside displays on the inside one of the popular decorative techniques of this ware. Here, two fish – symbols of fertility – have been moulded separately and then stuck to the bowl before glazing. Another version of the technique was to apply the moulded elements on top of the glaze so that they burnt red in the firing and provide a pleasing contrast to the green glaze.

9 Longquan *celadon bowl with fish in relief, Southern Song Dynasty (A.D. 1127-1279), diameter 13 cm (5⅛in); northern celadon bowl, Northern Song Dynasty (A.D. 960-1126).*

A small group of celadon dishes also featuring an opaque glaze was made in the 14th century during the Yuan Dynasty (A.D. 1260-1368). These dishes were completely moulded and all have elaborate

10 decoration similar to the one here, where the rim is bracket lobed and decorated with flowers; the well is also filled with flowers and its central medallion is occupied by some kind of mythical creature.

10 *Bowl, Korean, Koryŏ Dynasty, 12th-13th century, diameter 23.1cm (9⅛in); moulded dish, Yuan Dynasty, 1260-1368, diameter 16.8cm (6⅝in).*

Chinese celadon wares were much admired abroad, and their influence can be seen in the ceramics not only of Southeast Asia and the Near East but also, as evidenced by the small

10 conical bowl, of Korea. It is one of only two in the British Isles to display a particular Korean variant of celadon wares, for it is painted in copper red under the celadon glaze. It dates from the Koryŏ Dynasty of the 12th and 13th centuries A.D., when the Koreans experimented with various underglaze decorative techniques on celadon wares.

11 Jun *"bubble bowl", Song Dynasty, 12th century, diameter 10.1cm (4in).*

Wares related to the celadons were also made at both northern and southern Chinese kilns. In Zhejiang province, *guan* ware was produced, which at its finest had a very dark body and a widely crackled opaque blue-grey glaze. In the north, *ru* ware with its fine pale-buff body and thick opaque finely crackled blue-grey glaze ceased to be made after 1127 and has survived in very few examples. Another northern celadon relative, *jun*, was, like *ru*, an imperial ware during the Song Dynasty but it continued to be made well into the Ming Dynasty (1368-1644). The main kilns were scattered around Henan province, which accounts for the variety of body materials found among surviving examples. Some of the less good examples were not fired to as high a temperature as stoneware, but the better pieces were first fired unglazed to a low temperature and then glazed and fired to a higher temperature. *Jun* ware has an opaque ash glaze characterized by a great number of tiny bubbles, and is seen in a variety of blue tones achieved by the inclusion of iron oxide in the glaze and by reduction firing. Many of the surviving examples are bowls, and the small rounded version here,

11 known as a "bubble bowl", is particularly

representative. During the 12th century, the potters began to include splashes of copper to produce purplish-red streaks against the blue of the glaze, and, indeed, during the Ming Dynasty, large moulded pieces were made which were almost entirely red.

Black wares too were produced in both north and south China during the Song Dynasty. The northern or Henan black wares were made at least from the 10th to the 14th centuries, with a variety of bodies produced by a number of kilns. Typically, the body was first covered by a thick black slip – a sloppy clay and water mixture – containing quite a lot of iron oxide, and then glazed with a transparent brown glaze with less iron oxide, before firing in an oxidizing atmosphere to achieve the dense black colour. A variety of decorative techniques was adopted, including the one to be seen on the 13th-century **12** globular jar where the leaf decoration has been painted under the glaze in a slip

12 *Henan black-ware jar, Song Dynasty, 13th century, height 20.5cm (8⅛in).*

containing less iron oxide so that it turns rust-red when fired. A similar technique has been applied to one of the many tea bowls in **13** the Collection, which in this case displays a mottled effect of rust and black. Indeed, it is on the tea bowls that some of the best **13** decorative effects can be seen. On another, an attractive speckled glaze has been achieved

by using a period of reduction towards the end of the firing. The reducing atmosphere ensured that the excess iron in the black slip came up through the glaze in crystalline form to produce spots of metallic sheen. This **13** particular bowl has had its rim bound with

13 *Tea bowls: splashed design, Northern Song/Jin Dynasty; "hare's fur" glaze, Southern Song Dynasty (1127-1279); speckled glaze, Jin Dynasty; front: paper-cut design, Southern Song Dynasty, diameter 12.3cm (4⅞in).*

silver, a practice more often found on the "hare's fur"-glazed bowls made between the 11th and 14th centuries in the mountains of northern Fujian province. The practice arose because bowls of this type were taken back to Japan by Zen Buddhist monks who visited the area, but the Japanese found the rims too rough and so covered them with a band of silver. The body of these "hare's fur" pieces, products of the Jian kilns, is a very dark, coarse stoneware which is covered by a thick treacly glaze which tended to form a thick welt about two-thirds of the way down the outside. On the inside, the iron-oxide-rich glaze has run down to form a pool in the bottom of the bowl, producing the streaked, so-called hare's fur effect as it went.

The other black wares of the south are those made at kilns in the area of Jizhou in Jiangxi province between the 10th and 13th centuries. The body of these varies again from stoneware to porcelanous ware. One of the most interesting of the many decorative techniques employed on these Jizhou wares can be seen **13** on the tea bowl whose design has been produced by using paper-cuts. The paper-cut was stuck directly on the body which then had an iron-oxide glaze applied; finally, the piece was fired in a reducing atmosphere so that the carbons in the paper were left in the glaze to produce a dark-brown or black design against a speckled, fairly pale glaze. The tortoiseshell effect on the outside of the bowl was achieved by applying a yellow glaze over a black one.

The white wares of the Northern Song relied more for effect on the beauty of their glaze and the elegance of their form than on excessively complex decorative techniques. The classic *ding* wares, of which the Collection possesses a number of fine examples, were made in Hebei province from the late Tang Dynasty to the end of the 13th century, and found favour with the courts of the Northern Song and Jin Dynasties. The *ding* white wares have a very hard, white porcellanous body and a transparent ivory glaze with an orange tinge where it has run down the outside and formed what the Chinese call "tear stains". The most common shapes are dishes which were fired in saggers – fire-resistant boxes – upside down on their mouth rims, so that **14** these, as in the example here, have been

complex, and reminiscent of embroidery.

The best known of the white wares produced in the south during the Song Dynasty is *qingbai* – clear white – which continued to be produced into the 14th century and by that time had spawned some interesting and important variants of its glaze. It was made at Raozhou in northern Jiangxi province and had a sugary-white porcelain body with a transparent glaze of a slightly bluish tone which gave rise to its other name of *yinqing* – shadow blue. Like their northern *ding* counterparts, *qingbai* wares were made at first with incised decoration and then, in the second half of the 12th century, moulding was introduced for forming and decorating. The use of moulds considerably speeded up and simplified production and allowed some standardization, features which were important to the families and then the syndicates that, as early as the 13th century, owned and ran the kilns with a remarkably modern commercial attitude. The incised and carved designs continued, however, into the **15** 14th century. The Yuan Dynasty *meiping* –

14 Ding *ware dish, Northen Song Dynasty, 12th century, diameter 29.5cm (11⅜in).*

bound with a copper alloy, cut in one piece to avoid an unsightly join. The early *ding* wares were decorated with fluently drawn designs incised or carved under the glaze. As well as being freely drawn, these incised designs were very open and economical of line. The beginning of the 12th century, however, brought the introduction of another type of decoration of a very different style, created by placing the thrown bowl over a carved mould to produce a low relief, much more formal and

15 Meiping *vase, Yuan Dynasty, 14th century, height 27.3cm (10¾in).*

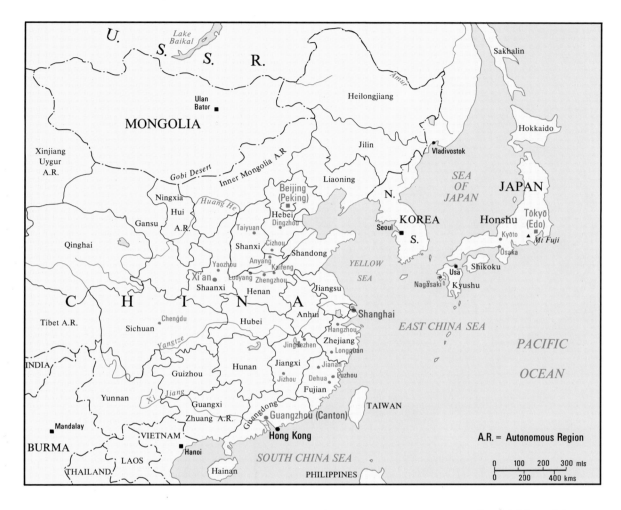

plum-blossom vase – with a freely carved dragon among waves providing its main decorative band, is a case in point. The division of the *meiping* vase shape into three distinct areas for the purpose of decoration was characteristic and favoured for many years to come.

In Jiangxi province, not far to the east of Raozhou City, is Jingdezhen, which was to become the most important centre of ceramic production in China, producing among others the wares for which the Chinese have become most famous – underglaze blue and white porcelains. The area was extremely well equipped to produce porcelain: fuel to fire the kilns was readily available; white clay – kaolin – could be dug from the nearby Gaoling hillside, from which it takes its name; and

baidunzi, or petuntse, a white feldspathic mineral which, when crushed, was mixed with kaolin to form the porcelain body, was also mined in the area. A relation of the *qingbai* glaze was used on these underglaze-blue porcelains and gave them a slight blue tinge which was regarded as quite acceptable right up to the 18th century, when a completely colourless glaze was demanded.

The process of underglaze decoration on porcelain is complicated by the fact that porcelain must be fired at over 1280 degrees centigrade and therefore there are only three colouring oxides that can be used: iron oxide, copper oxide and cobalt oxide. This last had been imported and used during the Tang Dynasty (A.D. 618-907) to colour lead glazes, but its use for underglaze decoration on

16 *Dish and bowl, Yuan Dynasty, 14th century, diameter of dish 46.3cm (18¼in), bowl 20.6cm (8⅛in); ewer, Ming Dynasty, 14th century, height 32.3cm (12¾in).*

porcelain posed quite different problems. The cobalt oxide itself came from the Near East, probably Kashan, where it had been used but where it had been found that it tended to run in the glaze. The Jingdezhen potters solved this problem by special preparation and application techniques and by the use of a very viscous glaze.

Many of the early blue and white pieces were made for the Near Eastern market, and indeed in its infancy the Chinese regarded this ornamental new technique as rather vulgar after the monochrome wares like *ding*, *qingbai* and the celadons. Hence, a number of the Yuan Dynasty 14th-century pieces, like the **16** large dish here, cater for Near Eastern requirements and are frequently based on Near Eastern metalwork forms. This dish has been made with a mould and has a deep well and a bracket-lobed rim. The design on the rim is interesting, however, for this particular wave pattern ties the plate to the two earliest

dated pieces of blue and white: the temple vases in the Percival David Foundation in London, dated by inscription to 1351.

Underglaze-red decoration, using copper oxide, was probably introduced at about the same time as the cobalt blue, and this was if anything an even more difficult material to control if the colour was to be preserved. The shapes and motifs were, however, the same as those found with the blue, and at the end of the 14th century more copper-red pieces seem to have been made than those with cobalt-blue decoration. This may be attributable to a shortage of cobalt at that time, due to the ports being closed and foreign trade limited at the beginning of the Ming Dynasty. There are two examples of this early **16** copper-red ware in the Collection: a bowl with peony scroll inside and chrysanthemum scroll **16** outside; and a very handsome ewer with an ogival panel filled with peony scrolls and a cloud-shaped strut joining its slender spout to

17 *Tankard, Ming Dynasty, early 15th century, height 18.7cm (7⅜in).*

18 Kraak porselein *bowl, late 16th–early 17th century, diameter 21.5cm (8½in).*

19 *Square box, Wanli period (1573–1619), width 26.6cm (10½in).*

the neck. Although the overall decorative effect is very ornate, the skill with which the artist has tailored the various elements to compliment the difficult shape of the ewer is quite remarkable. The purely Chinese decorative elements like the floral scrolls have been used well, while the imported motifs like the cloud-collar have been thoughtfully adapted.

An example of a purely Near Eastern design being used almost unchanged on a piece of blue and white or red and white ware can be seen in the charming early 15th-century blue and white tankard. Its form has been taken from a Near Eastern metalwork shape, and the peculiar lattice design on the domed lid has also been borrowed from the Near East. It is interesting, too, to compare the wave design on the neck of this tankard with that on the rim of the dish, to see how it had developed since the mid-14th century.

While underglaze-red decoration declined in popularity, underglaze blue went from strength to strength, and an indigenous supply of cobalt was located in Yunnan and began gradually to come into use after 1426. The designs were by now well adapted to Chinese taste, and the exported wares were going even farther afield than the Near East.

18 The deep bowl here is of a type known as *kraak porselein* which belongs to the late 16th or early 17th centuries. It was exported to Southeast Asia and Indonesia and was also brought to Europe in the 17th century. It owes its name to the Dutch pronunciation of the name for the Portuguese galleons, or carracks, which carried porcelain from China to Indonesia. One of these was captured by the Dutch on her outward voyage in 1603, and the name was coined and used thereafter. The decoration of this ware is usually in a rather watery cobalt blue, and the motifs are mainly of plants and animals, frequently the spotted deer as on this bowl. It is also characteristic of the design that it is divided into radiating panels. The body of these wares is of quite good quality, but it is often very thin for the size of the vessels, and the glaze, like that on many examples of 17th-century porcelain, is not a good "fit" on the body so that it tends to break away at the rim, a feature known as "tender edges".

A much more solidly constructed example

of blue and white ware of about the same period, the reign of Wanli (1573-1619), can be
19 seen in the large square box with lobed corners. The decoration on this is much more formal and more precisely drawn. The motifs are also interesting, the main one being the imperial five-clawed dragon. On the top of the lid, two of these confront each other above the standard configuration of mountains, waves and clouds. The rest of the motifs are all linked to longevity: the character *shou,* meaning longevity, is inscribed on a peach – a symbol of longevity – and is flanked on either side by elaborate *lingzhi,* the sacred fungus, which is also symbolic of longevity. The same fungus is also used as a scroll on the edges of both the base and lid of the box.

In addition to the superb blue and white porcelains produced during the Ming Dynasty (1368-1644), a number of other polychrome effects were introduced which are well represented in the Collection. The
20 lovely writhing green dragon on the dish, for instance, is an attractive example of a combination of on-the-biscuit and overglaze enamel. The design for the dragon and clouds was incised into the body and then painted with wax. The rest of the dish was covered by glaze and the dish was then fired, curing the glaze and burning away the wax. Green enamel was then applied onto the unglazed area of the dragon and clouds, but the extra details of the claws and the flames were painted on over the glaze. Finally, the dish

20 *Dish with dragon, Hongzhi reign (1488-1505), diameter 20cm (7⅞in); lobed ewer and cover, c.1600, height 19cm (7½in).*

was fired again at a lower temperature. This dish has the reign mark of Hongzhi (1488-1505) inscribed on the base in underglaze blue, indicating within which emperor's reign it was made.

20 The charming little lobed ewer, dating from about 1600, provides an example of a rather different use of overglaze enamels. This is decorated in *wucai* – five-colour – enamels which were often combined, as in this case, with underglaze-blue designs. In this technique, some of the design was applied under the glaze – on the ewer this includes the *shou* (longevity) character, some details of the dragon and sections of the decorative bands as well as the outlines of the lobes. The vessel was then glazed and fired, and the overglaze enamels applied – on this piece red, yellow, brown, green and black. Here, as in other examples of the technique, the outlines of the decoration have been drawn in either red or black. On this little ewer, the lobed form has been emphasized by using each lobe as a decorative panel with a different flowering or fruiting branch springing alternately from the top or bottom of the panel.

The on-the-biscuit technique of enamel decoration was developed in a particularly attractive ware known as *fahua* which also appeared during the Ming Dynasty. The technique worked on a principle similar to that of metalwork cloisonné enamel, but in porcelains the individual motifs were outlined in a thin relief line drawn in slip and have some details incised. The vessel was fired and then the coloured glazes were applied within the raised lines. One of the favourite shapes
21 of *fahua* ware is the *guan* jar like the one here, which also has a characteristic use of colours with cobalt blue and turquoise predominating. The choice of motifs is also typical, with clouds around the neck, strings of jewels on the shoulders, birds and flowers in landscape as the main decorative band, and waves around the lower section.

This enamel-on-biscuit technique can be seen in a very different context on the large,
22 almost life-size, figure of a seated Buddhist *lohan* – a disciple – also illustrated at the beginning of this chapter. Here we see a return to the palette of the Tang polychrome wares – green, cream and yellow/amber – and, indeed, these later polychromes are

sometimes known as "Ming *sancai*". The figure sits in serene contemplation, cross-legged, his hands folded in his lap. The robes are of simple cut, but are edged with an ornate floral border, and the green outer robe still retains traces of gilt decoration. We know quite a lot about this figure, for on the side of **22** his rocky pedestal is an inscription which has been translated thus:

"Chenghua twentieth year [1484] mid-autumn. Made on an auspicious day, the believer Wang Jin-ao, his wife Miaojin and his son Wang Qin and the priest Daoji. The workman Liuzhen."

Hence, we know the name of the man who made it and for whom, as well as when it was dedicated and the name of the officiating priest.

The technique was not, however, restricted to such august subjects, or even to porcelain.
23 The pouncing lion with his curly green mane

21 Guan *jar with* fahua *enamels*, c.1500, height 30.4cm (12in).

22 *Details of head and inscription, polychrome* **lohan** *figure, 1484, height 127cm (50in).*

23 *Lion roof tile, 16th-17th century, 22.2×41.9cm (8¾×16½in).*

24 *Demon roof tile, 16th-17th century, 42.5×25.4cm (16¾×10in).*

25 *Armoured guardian figures, Ming Dynasty, 14th century, height 24.1cm (9½in).*

24 and the fierce-faced demon are both made of stoneware and are in fact roof tiles. Many of the important buildings of China in the past had roofs made of brightly coloured ceramic tiles. The end tiles along the ridges often had, and still have on existing buildings, various figures standing on them to ward off evil spirits. Our lion and demon are two of these.

Two guardians of a rather more formal type **25** are the armoured figures in their winged helmets. These are Ming Dynasty pieces of *longquan* celadon and are effective examples of green-glazed areas contrasting with elaborately moulded areas which have been left unglazed and have therefore turned red when fired. Their armour has been shown in considerable detail, even down to the writhing dragons on their breastplates.

In addition to these colourful pieces, the Collection also contains excellent examples of Ming and Qing monochrome wares. While many of these rely for effect on the beauty of **27** their glaze, there are some like the small bowl here which are just as elaborate in their own

26 *Copper-red bowl, Xuande period (1426-35), diameter 18.4cm (7¼in); cobalt-blue dish, Jiajing period (1522-66), diameter 21.5cm (8½in); yellow dish, Kangxi period (1662-1722), diameter 27.6cm (10⅞in).*

way as their more colourful counterparts. This early 17th-century bowl is decorated with openwork in a trellis design, known as *linglong* or "Devil's work", and when in use it would have had a silver lining. The five openwork medallions which punctuate the trellis depict Daoist immortals in complex relief.

26 The deep-blue dish does rely for its effect on the beauty of its cobalt glaze and the perfect

27 Linglong *bowl, early 17th century, diameter 9.5cm (3¾in).*

balance of its form. This dish, which has on its base the mark of Jiajing (1522-66) has no decoration and needs none. The same can be **26** said of the bowl with the copper-red glaze. In the early 15th century, potters learned to control this very difficult colorant and produced vessels with a lovely deep-red glaze which usually has a slight "orange peel" texture and a pure white rim. The copper glaze is covered by a colourless glaze, and it is where this second glaze runs away from the rim that the copper glaze is exposed and volatilizes, leaving the rim white. This bowl bears the reign mark of Xuande (1426-35) on its base and, unlike many others similarly marked, is actually of that period. A monochrome copper-red glaze was reintroduced in the 17th century, at the beginning of the Qing dynasty (1644-1912), but, as can be seen from various examples in the Collection, it was rather different in nature from the 15th-century pieces. On these later examples, the unglazed porcelain was fired first, then the two glazes were added and the

28 *Trumpet-mouth vase and peach-bloom water pot, Kangxi period (1662-1722), height of vase 20.9cm (8¼in).*

29 Famille verte *lautern, Kangxi period (1622-1722), height 22.8cm (9in).*

vessel was fired again at an even higher temperature, resulting in a very glossy glaze with fine crazing and a pale shadow running down from the rim. This later red is known as *langyao, sang de boeuf,* or oxblood – the same name, but three different languages.

Another monochrome colour popular both in the Ming and Qing Dynasties was yellow, the imperial colour. The precise tone of the yellow depended on a number of factors, including whether the antimony glaze was applied directly to the body or was applied as an enamel over an existing colourless glaze.
26 The shallow dish shown, which has the reign mark of Kangxi (1662-1722) incised on the base under the glaze, also has a design incised under the glaze on the inside of the vessel, depicting three fruit – peach, pomegranate and finger citrus – which symbolize the Three Abundances of years, sons and happiness.

A much admired variant of the copper-red glaze, which appeared in the 18th century, is known in the West as peach-bloom and in China as *pingguo hong* – apple red. The colour was a subtle pinkish red that mottled and turned green in places, and since the glaze effect involved extremely careful control of kiln conditions, it was very expensive to produce. Only eight shapes are known to have been made with peach-bloom glaze, and all these are small, suitable for placement on a
28 scholar's table. The beehive-shaped water pot is a prime example, and close examination reveals finely incised decorative roundels

28 under the glaze. The small vase gives some indication of just how much these pieces were prized, for it has obviously been broken at some time but has been mended most beautifully around the mouth in silver gilt, and the mend across the body has even been made into a flower stem with the centres of the flowers being the rivets.

Perhaps the best-known development in 18th-century polychrome ware was the introduction of an opaque purplish-pink enamel. Derived from colloidal gold, it became incorporated into a type of decoration of opaque and transluscent enamels, known as *famille rose.* Although Sir William Burrell did purchase some of the wares decorated in this way, he sold them again; no one seems to know why. He did, however, keep some of the items decorated in the *famille noire* style, with their dramatic black backgrounds and white panels decorated with coloured enamels. But it is the pieces with *famille verte* decoration that he favoured most. The lantern
29 dating from the Kangxi period (1662-1722) shows these translucent enamels to full advantage. As the name suggests, clear greens predominate in the palette but with the addition of aubergine, blue and occasional touches of opaque iron red and black. As with many pieces of the period, the design shows figures in a domestic setting, while the

30 *Tree-shrew water pot and lotus-pod ewer, Kangxi period (1662-1722), height of ewer 13.6cm (5⅜in).*

decorative bands include items from among the Eight Buddhist Emblems and the Eight Precious Things.

The Qing Dynasty, and especially the reign of the Kangxi emperor, saw the production of many small, rather charming pieces **30** of naturalistic form, coloured with on-the-biscuit enamels. The small ewer in the shape of a lotus pod is typical of the way in which natural shapes were adapted, while the **30** delightful little tree shrew with leaf and berries in his mouth would once again have graced the scholar's table as a water pot.

Although introduced in the Tianqi period (1621-27), it was only during Kangxi's long and artistically rich reign that the so-called powder-blue wares were fully established. To produce this speckled effect, cobalt blue was blown through a bamboo tube with gauze over the end onto the body of the vessel before glazing. The resulting glaze was sometimes left plain or, as can be seen on the handsome **31** rouleau vase, gilded decoration was added to the surface. On occasion, areas were left white for the application of overglaze enamels like those used for the magnificent carp on this vase. Gilding was also applied to the plain black vases produced at the time, but on both these and powder-blue ware it tended to be very fugitive and has not survived well.

Considerable quantities of Chinese ceramics were exported to Europe during the Qing Dynasty, many with designs copied from drawings sent from Europe and many in specifically European shapes. Once they arrived in Europe, these pieces were often embellished; in this case a Dutch silver mount **32** has been added to a chocolate cup which features a rather uninspired blue and white decoration of ladies in a garden.

Very fine underglaze-blue painting is still to be found, however, during the reign of the emperor Qianlong (1736-95) who, like his

31 *Powder-blue rouleau vase, Kangxi period (1662-1722), height 44.7cm (17⅜in).*

32 *Blue and red bowl, Qianlong period (1736-95), diameter 22.5cm (8⅞in); blue and white chocolate cup, Kangxi period (1662-1722).*

ancestor the Kangxi emperor, had a long reign during which he was an indefatigable patron **32** of the arts. A bowl here displays a very high quality of underglaze-blue painting, combining it skilfully with underglaze copper red, and with a well-controlled overglaze rose enamel highlighting the waves. Inside, Shoulao, the god of longevity, is depicted, while on the outside are the Eight Daoist Immortals, each identifiable by what he or she carries and rides upon across the waves.

Chinese Bronzes

The bronze vessels of ancient China are perhaps less readily appreciated by the western eye than, say, the ceramics; but they have been prized for centuries by the Chinese themselves for their variety of elegant forms and their intricate decoration, evincing as they do the skill of the early craftsmen. They have also been prized for their patina, the subtle colouring built up by years of exposure to the air, which ranges from blackish brown to a brilliant blue-green and has always been one of the aspects of an ancient bronze most valued by the Chinese connoisseur, as indeed it appears to have been by Sir William Burrell.

Items made of bronze, an alloy of copper and tin, have been found in small numbers at archaeological sites in China dating from about 2300-2000 B.C., but cast-bronze items do not appear in any number until the era which the Chinese call the period of the Erlitou culture, the 19th to 16th centuries B.C., and which they associate with the legendary Xia Dynasty mentioned in historical texts. The height of the bronze-caster's art, however, was reached during the Shang and Zhou Dynasties (16th-11th centuries B.C. and 11th-3rd centuries B.C., respectively), and it is from these periods that the majority of the bronzes in the Collection date.

The bronzes made during the Shang and Western Zhou (1027-771 B.C.) periods were all cast using piece moulds. A clay model of the required object was made, including the carved decoration, then the sections of the mould were made around it, taking into account the mortices and tenons necessary to join the pieces of the mould together. The core of the mould was then made so that the gap between the inner and outer sections would be the thickness of the finished vessel, while a hole was left to enable the molten bronze to be poured in. The pieces of the mould were then fired to become porous pottery. The fact that the moulds were porous was important as this allowed air bubbles trapped in the molten bronze to escape and so produced sharper details of decoration. Sandstone moulds have been found at some Shang sites, but these would have been less satisfactory. The

1 Jue, *Shang Dynasty, 15th-13th century B.C., height 18cm (7⅜in).*
2 *Detail of* taotie *mask on* jue.

lost-wax method of bronze-casting, which was used for early bronze-making in Europe, does not appear to have been used in China until about the 5th century B.C.

Most of the objects that have survived from these early periods are ritual vessels, but some weapons have been found and a very few tools. Nevertheless, we know from the large number of tool moulds that have been found at bronze-casting centres that a considerable number of these were made. The paucity of existing examples is less surprising if we remember, on the one hand, that bronze was a valuable metal that could be melted down and used again, and on the other, that most of the extant bronzes have come from the tombs of the ruling classes where ritual vessels would

3 Fu, *Zhou Dynasty, 8th century B.C., width 29.8cm (11¾in);* xian *steamer, late Shang or early Zhou Dynasty, 11th century B.C., height 38.7cm (15¼in).*

be far more likely to be deposited than tools.

Ritual sacrifice, especially to ancestors, was an important part of the life of the ruling classes during the Shang and Zhou periods, and the rituals that individuals were allowed to perform were determined by their social position. During the Shang Dynasty, the ritual bronzes were made for the king and his ministers to use, but with the dissipation of the power of the king during the Zhou Dynasty many ritual vessels were made for the powerful feudal lords.

Although it is not possible to identify from the ancient texts all the different types of ritual vessels and their precise purpose, we are able to say with a fair degree of certainty whether a vessel was to be used for food, wine or water. **1** *Jues,* such as the one illustrated, were – as their spouts suggest – used for wine. An inscription of two characters appears under the handle on the side of this *jue.* These short inscriptions are common on bronzes of this period (15th-13th centuries B.C.) and usually give the family name of the owner or identify the deceased. Long inscriptions are found occasionally on vessels of the late Shang period (13th-11th centuries B.C.), but it is not until the Zhou period that lengthy inscriptions such as

descriptions of historical events occur with any regularity.

The decorative band around the body of the *jue* includes the most popular of all the bronze **2** motifs, the *taotie* mask, found in many forms on the bronzes, and indeed on the jades, of several centuries. The abstract mask is in two halves, each half on either side of a central flange being a mirror image of the other. The eyes predominate, but it is possible also to trace ears, eyebrows, horns and the rest of the body so that each half can also be seen as a whole animal viewed in profile. It has been suggested that this monster mask was based on an ox or a tiger. One curious feature is that the beast has only an upper jaw – hence the idea that it is a glutton, having eaten its own lower jaw. Another type of mask features the mirror images of two dragons, apparently two-legged and standing on their noses, one on either side of a central flange. These masks, along with the birds that became increasingly popular during the Zhou period, are the main motifs on ancient Chinese bronzes. Masks modelled in relief are also a frequent embellishment, especially above the handles, as is the case on this *jue.*

3   A bronze vessel of a very different shape

provides an example of the way the mask was adapted to the surfaces of different vessel forms. The tall, waisted tripod is called a *xian* and is a steamer for food, with a hinged, perforated tray inside it. On this example from the late Shang or early Zhou period of the 11th century B.C., it is possible to see that the *taotie* mask of the upper decorative band is composed of abstract scroll-like devices whereas the masks at the top of the pouched legs have the facial features clearly delineated.

4   Another food vessel, this time called a *gui,* from the early Western Zhou period, shows the *taotie* mask again in the central band, while individual dragons provide the upper and lower decorative bands, and high-relief masks surmount the handles and the *taotie's* central flange. Beside it, and also from the Western

4 Zhou period, is a vessel for wine – a sort of small bucket with lid – called a *you* which has the mask in the same position on the band but with no flange below it. On either side are elaborately crested, long-tailed birds against a background of scrolls, called *lei wen,* or thunder pattern, and the device is repeated on the lid. The animal heads on the handle of this *you* are clearly neither those of ox nor tiger but well-modelled deer.

A rather strange 8th-century B.C. vessel that was used for food, and also possibly for

3 storage, is the *fu.* It has a rectangular section, and the two halves are almost identical so that the lid may be turned over to form a separate receptacle like the base. The relief masks appear again on the handles and rim, but the main decoration is formed by writhing dragons with entangled bodies but whose heads can be identified by their eyes and upturned noses.

5   The lidded *hu* of the Eastern Zhou, Warring States period was also used for wine and has bands of decoration that look at first sight to be completely abstract. Closer inspection reveals, however, that the design is made up of eyes and the writhing forms of dragons. The dragons on the lid are easier to discern, while a double-headed reptile provides the handle joining the chains by which the *hu* could be carried.

A debased version of the decoration seen on

5 the *hu* also appears on one of the bells in the Collection, which is of similar date. This bell, like all early Chinese bells, is elliptical in cross-section and clapperless, and is played by striking it with a bronze or wooden hammer. The bells were designed to emit two different notes depending on where they are struck, and are often part of a set of bells suspended from a wooden frame. The most extensive set that has been excavated so far,

4 *Lidded* you, *Western Zhou Dynasty, 10th century* B.C., *height 20.9cm (8 ¼in);* gui, *early Western Zhou Dynasty, 11th century* B.C., *13.3 ×28.5cm (5 ¼×11 ¼in).*

5 *Bell, Eastern Zhou, Warring States period, 5th century* B.C., *height 31.7cm (12½in); lidded* **hu,** *Eastern Zhou, Warring States period, 5th-4th century* B.C., *height 34.2cm (13½in).*
6 Lian *from the Kingdom of Dian, 2nd-1st century* B.C., *51.4×57.1cm (20¼in×22½in).*

consisting of sixty-five bells, was unearthed from the tomb of a nobleman at Suixian in Hubei province and, like the Burrell bell, is from the Warring States period.

One of the largest and finest pieces in the Collection is a *lian* – a cylindrical box. Most *lian* are designed to hold mirrors, combs and cosmetics, but the size of this one suggests some sort of storage vessel. Apart from the masks holding the ring handles, the decoration is entirely different from that on the other bronzes, for this piece from the 2nd or 1st centuries B.C. comes from the southeast, almost certainly from the site of Shizhaishan in the Kingdom of Dian in what is now Yunnan province. Human figures are rare on bronzes, but the feet of this *lian* are in the form of crouching men. The decorative bands are also completely different in style from those of the other bronzes here. They are in low relief with geometric bands top and bottom and

three other bands in between: one of flying cranes; one of standing birds, possibly hornbills; and one of spotted deer, alternately male and female. All go in procession anticlockwise around the *lian*.

The Collection also has a number of later bronzes from the Han Dynasty (206 B.C.-A.D. 220) to the Qing (A.D. 1644-1911). The bronze vessels of the Warring States and Han periods were popular with collectors of later centuries and were the inspiration for items that were produced in a deliberately archaistic style. Two good examples of this archaistic style are a Song Dynasty (A.D. 690-1279) *hu* vase inlaid with gold and silver in imitation of a Warring States' period vessel and a Song-Ming period "champion vase", similar in design and function to the example in jade discussed on page 68, which copies Shang and Zhou Dynasty decorative schemes.

7 **Hu** *inlaid with gold and silver, Song Dynasty (A.D.960-1279), height 25.4cm (10in); "champion vase", Song or Ming Dynasty, height 27.9cm (11in).*

Chinese Furniture

Chinese furniture is a relatively new field of acquisition for The Burrell Collection, with Sir William Burrell's Trustees together with the assistance of the National Art Collections Fund, purchasing a number of 16th-17th century Ming period pieces of hardwood furniture in 1993.

The 16th-17th centuries are considered to be the golden age of Chinese furniture-making, when both design and construction were of a particularly high standard. Furniture-making was carried on throughout China, but there were a number of centres that specialised in the production of furniture, the most important being the wealthy and fashionable city of Suzhou and the port city of Canton. The most popular wood for cabinet-making was *huanghuali* wood, which can range in colour from a pale yellow (as the Chinese name suggests), to a purplish red. It is a hardwood, related to the Pterocarpus or Dalbergia family, with a beautiful grain and emits a strong fragrance when sawn. Varieties of huanghuali were traditionally sourced in South China and imported from India and South-east Asia.

Ming period furniture makers fully understood the concept of form and function and always designed and constructed furniture that was both practical and visually attractive. No nails or screws were used in manufacture and very little glue. So sophisticated is the construction of

1 Chinese furniture that the square table in the Collection can easily be dismantled and reassembled. Square tables were often placed against walls and under windows and sometimes in the centre of a room with stools on all four sides. Tables of all shapes were used for a variety of purposes, from dining to writing.

2 The Yokeback chair, like the table, is not restricted in its use. It might have been placed beside another chair of the same design, or positioned at the side of a table as it is here. The Chinese call these chairs *meiguiyi* and they are characterised by rectangular arms and back and a general compactness.

1 *Square table.*

2 *Yokeback chair.*

Chinese Jades

Jade has always been considered by the Chinese to be a very special material. In Neolithic times it was obviously highly prized for its hardness which made it ideal for tools and weapons. In later periods it was valued for its aesthetic qualities, not only visual but tactile, and also for the mystical properties that were attributed to it. These included the prevention of bodily decay, and hence jade funerary suits were made for some members of the aristocracy. Less extravagantly, small jade plaques were attached to shrouds, crescent-shaped pendants were placed on the breast, and small jade items were used to plug the corpse's orifices, among them small jade cicadas which were traditionally placed on the tongues of the dead.

The high regard in which jade has always been held in China is evidenced by the fact that the Chinese word for jade, *yu,* if used adjectivally can also imply pure, precious, or even noble or royal. Geologically, the term ''jade'' is used very loosely in China and can be applied to any valuable, hard, workable stone, while in the West the two minerals to which it is applied are nephrite and jadeite. The latter, however, was not imported into China in any quantity until the 18th century so most of the items in the Collection are of nephrite or one of the other hard stones. Nephrite, too, was mainly imported, for there are no known sources near the main centres of habitation in China, and the primary areas from which it came were Khotan and Yarkand in central Asia and the region around Lake Baikal in eastern Siberia.

The material presents considerable problems for the lapidary who seeks to shape and decorate it, as nephrite is a silicate of calcium, magnesium and aluminium (sometimes with the addition of iron), which has undergone a metamorphosis caused by heat or pressure so that its hair-like crystals become felted together to form a closely packed mass. This produces a stone which is tougher than steel. Jade cannot therefore be carved in the usual sense of the word, but must be abraded, using tools that have been armed with some sort of strong abrasive. In

early times this would have been quartz sand. Later, crushed almandine garnets were used, and later still, crushed corundum, while of course in this century Carborundum has become available. Until the middle of the present century, the tools used by jade lapidaries had changed very little over the centuries, with instruments like bamboo drills powered by hand still in use in Beijing – Peking – as late as the 1930s.

The Burrell Collection includes jade objects dating from the Neolithic period, the Bronze Age and through to the last dynasty of China, the Qing (1644-1912). Among the different types of object are weapons, items for ritual use, personal ornaments, funerary objects, vessels and small human and animal figures.

Some of the most interesting jade weapons are those dating from the Bronze Age of China and especially those of the Shang (*c.*1600-1027 B.C.) and the Zhou Dynasties (1027-221 B.C.). Some items, such as sword slides, which were attached about two-thirds of the way up a scabbard to allow it to be hung from a belt, were suitable for general use while others were obviously intended only for ritual or ceremonial purposes. Two of the finest examples of the latter, which combine the art of the lapidary and that of the bronze-caster,

1 are a ceremonial axe and a ceremonial halberd blade and its tang, both dating from the late

1 *Axe with jade blade and jade halberd blade with bronze tang, Shang Dynasty, 13th-11th century* B.C. *Length of axe 13.9cm (5½in).*

Shang Dynasty (13th-11th centuries B.C.). The handle of the axe and the tang of the halberd are made of bronze and the former is inlaid with turquoise. Both reflect designs found on bronze vessels of the period.

2   Jade pendants are frequently in the shapes of birds, fish or dragons. Those in the Collection include a particularly fine example with a dragon's head at either end, which dates from the Warring States period of the Zhou Dynasty. The majority of the pendants in the Collection are datable to the Bronze Age, the Shang, Zhou and Han Dynasties, but there are also later examples, illustrated alongside, which adopt the same subject but treat it differently, as in the Song Dynasty example of a fish which has been coiled round to bite its own tail, thus forming a circle.

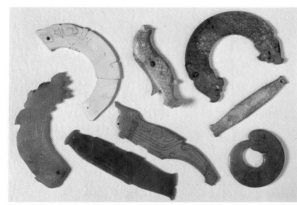

2 *Pendants and plaques, various periods, diameter of fish 5cm (2in).*

In addition to weapons for ritual or ceremonial use, two other objects are frequently found in jade and are undoubtedly of ritual significance. The first of these is called a *zong* and is basically a cylinder with a square outside perimeter and a round inside. The height is variable, and they are sometimes smooth and sometimes notched on the square outer face, the notches of the earlier examples deriving from a face or mask. Their precise function in the ancient rituals is not clear, but the form is generally regarded as the symbol of the Earth.

The other very popular ritual form is the *bi*, of which we have several examples in the Collection, covering a number of different periods and with a range of different decorative treatments. The *bi* is a flat, circular

3 **Bi** *with shallow carving, Han Dynasty, 3rd-1st century B.C., diameter 17.1cm (6¾in).*

4 **Bi** *with felines, Han Dynasty (206B.C.-A.D.220), diameter 22.8cm (9in).*

5 *Rhyton, 13th–15th century* A.D., *height 13.9cm (5½in).*

6 *"Champion vase", 13th–15th century* A.D., *height 9.5cm (3¾in).*

object with a hole in the centre, and although again its exact significance is not certain, it is most probably a symbol of Heaven and was used for presentation to or by the emperor, who was known as the Son of Heaven.

3 A particularly fine example of a *bi* from the 3rd to the 1st centuries B.C. has on its inside decorative band a pattern of slightly raised comma-shapes which are characteristic of this period, while four shallowly carved, intertwined dragons form the outside band. The faces of the dragons are reminiscent of the *taotie* masks seen on early bronzes but have been adapted to suit the different medium.

Writhing creatures also provide the

4 decoration for a large, heavier *bi* of the Han Dynasty, but unlike the previous example these three felines are in high relief with quite separate, clearly defined limbs. Felines of the sort seen on this *bi* are very popular in decorative schemes of the Han Dynasty and continued to find their way into the

ornamentation of later dynasties as well, often as part of the Chinese tradition of conscious

5 archaism. The rhyton – a drinking vessel – of the 13th to 15th centuries A.D. has vigorously carved examples of these felines clambering up its sides, their forepaws reaching for the rim, and peering into the cup. The creatures are in very high relief, while the cup itself is covered with a finely incised design.

This combination of a high-relief creature on a vessel decorated with low-relief designs is a familiar one among jades and can be seen again on one of the finest pieces in the

6 Collection, a "champion vase" of similar date to the rhyton. So-called champion vases are also found in bronze (indeed there is a fine example in the Collection, illustrated on page 65), and it is thought that they may have been awarded in archery contests. The name itself involves a play on words. All these vases are composed of two cylinders held together by the wingspan of an eagle standing on a bear.

7 *Recumbent beast, 13th-15th century* A.D.; *seated beast, Ming Dynasty, height 7.6cm (3in); ornament of two melons, Qing Dynasty, 18th century* A.D.

The Chinese words for "eagle" and "bear" are *ying* and *xiong*. The word for "hero" or "champion", although the written form is different, is also pronounced *yingxiong*, hence the name. There is also the possibility of a pun on the flight of an arrow.

The Collection, of course, also includes examples of very elegant jade vases and bowls which rely for their attraction as much on the way the markings of the original stone have been brought out by the lapidary as on their surface decoration or lovely shape. But this appreciation of the intrinsic qualities of the stone can perhaps be seen at its best in the small in-the-round carvings of animals, figures and fruit. The large-eyed and rather
7 appealing beast with its head turned back over its body shows well how the craftsman has not only used the colours in the stone but has almost certainly been guided by the original shape of the pebble when deciding on the form of the creature. The same criteria have

7 influenced the design of the two melons with their vines and leaves, butterflies and bats. The inclusion of bats in the decoration of this piece – and in many other examples of the decorative arts in China, especially during the Qing Dynasty (1644-1912), the period to which the melon group belongs – is evidence yet again of the Chinese love of puns. Because the word for "bat", *fu,* is pronounced in the same way as the word for happiness, the bat has become a symbol of felicity or good fortune and thus a popular decorative motif.

An aspect of these small pieces that is often forgotten by those in the West but has traditionally been appreciated by the Chinese is how they feel – these lovely little figures were not only to be looked at but held. The
7 charming little seated creature of Ming Dynasty date (1368-1644) fits perfectly into the palm of the hand, feeling cool and smooth, appealing to the sense of touch as well as being visually attractive.

Japanese Prints

Japanese prints do not appear to have been imported into Europe until the early 19th century – and the first of these may well have arrived as wrapping for other objects. Indeed, they did not achieve much general appreciation before their appearance at the International Exhibition in London in 1862. Since that time, however, they have gained tremendous popularity in the West and have had a considerable influence on various aspects of Western art, not least commercial art – theatre posters and the like – at the end of the 19th and the beginning of the 20th century.

The art of the Japanese print is to a large extent the art of *ukiyo-e* – pictures of the floating or transitory world – which took as its primary theme the life of the Yoshiwara – the licensed entertainment quarter of Edo (modern Tokyo) – or its equivalent in the cities of Osaka, Kyōto and Nagasaki. From the 17th to the 19th centuries, the *ukiyo-e* artists both in paintings and prints depicted the world of the courtesan and, with the development of Kabuki drama in the 18th century, that of the theatre. Themes taken from the popular literature of the time and from history are also frequently represented among Japanese prints, as are certain semi-religious and legendary figures as well as famous Japanese landscape features such as Mount Fuji.

The prints in the Collection all date from the 18th and 19th centuries – when the art of the printmaker had reached its maturity and the subtler techniques had been developed – and all are figure subjects. Most of the famous print artists are represented, including Kunisada, Utamaro, Kuniyoshi and Hokusai. Sir William seems to have been particularly fond of Hokusai, as there are a number of his works in the Collection, including a print dated 1835, of the artist himself disguised as an old fisherman smoking his pipe.

1 Katsushika Hokusai (1760-1849) was an extremely versatile artist and the style of the self portrait is in considerable contrast to an earlier print of about 1816 which

2 shows a courtesan, her hair elaborately dressed and wearing a beautiful kimono 'making a parade' for which she adopts a particular, formal style of walking – a formality which is reflected in the use of the Chinese Han Dynasty clerical script for the accompanying inscription.

The self portrait of Hokusai is a *surimono*, that is a small high quality print produced for a special occasion such as a marriage, a birthday or the New Year. More than half the prints in the Collection are *surimono* which are characterised by delicate printing enhanced by embossed designs in the paper and the use of various metal dusts. All these aspects are used in the print by Aoigaoka

3 Hokkei (1780-1850), the subject of which is taken from *Chusingura* or 'Loyal League of Forty-seven Ronin', a popular drama about a group of masterless samurai warriors and the subject of a considerable number of prints. This print depicts the samurai Wakasa, who has cut off a pine tree branch with the words: "Thus may the enemies of my lord perish by his hand." It dates from about 1825.

1 *Katsushika Hokusai* Old Fisherman Smoking His Pipe, *c.1835, 21.5×18.4cm (8½×7¼in).*

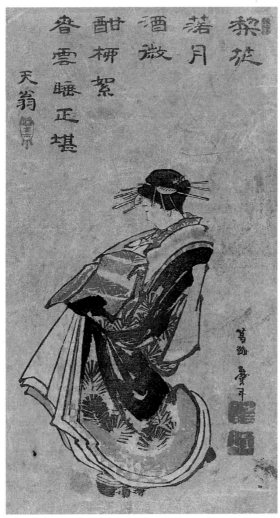

2 *Katsushika Hokusai* Courtesan Making A Parade, c.1816, 35.5×16.5cm (14×6½in).

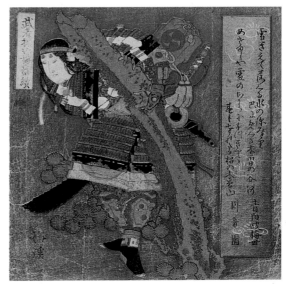

3 *Aoigaoka Hokkei* Armed Warrior With Pine Tree Branch, c.1825, 21.5×18.4cm (8½×7¼in).

4 *Utagawa Kunisada* Shōki The Demon Queller, c.1849-53, 35.8×24.1cm (14×9½in).

One of the most popular legendary figures depicted in print form was Shōki, the demon queller. He is seen here in a dramatic print by Utagawa Kunisada (1786-1865) in characteristically fierce pose, flourishing his sword with one arm and holding an *oni* – a demon – under the other. The print bears a number of red seals; the artist's (bottom right), the publisher (bottom left) and the two censors who approved publication, Hama and Magomi, which appear above the artist's signature and which date the print to between 1849 and 1853.

Central Asian Embroideries

Central Asian embroideries in the Collection number eleven hangings – *suzani* – from Uzbekistan and two from West Turkestan. In addition there are five hangings from Turkey and one from Northwest Persia. Sir William seems to have purchased them to furnish his and Lady Burrell's home, Hutton Castle, for many contemporary photographs show a number of them masquerading as bedspreads. However, they would originally have been made as wall hangings, interior curtains or covers for a typical Uzbek household. The term *suzani* is a Tadzhik word meaning an embroidered cloth and usually consists of floss silk manufactured locally, embroidered on to an undyed and unbleached cotton fabric called *buz*. The work was carried out by women who would spend years on embroideries for their houses and – in the case of unmarried women – their dowries.

Most surviving *suzani* date from the late 19th century, when Russian control of Central Asia encouraged the expansion of trade and the economic exploitation of cotton. It was at this time that Uzbek embroidered cloths were first really appreciated in the West. The main centres of Uzbek domestic embroidery were **1, 2, 3** Bukhara, Nurata, Shakhrisabz, Samarkand, Tashkent and Fergana and the first three are represented in the Burrell Collection.

The decorative scheme of the embroideries follows closely that of the average oriental carpet; a large central field surrounded by a narrow border. Very often the border itself is edged by an even narrower inner and outer band. All the *suzani*-producing areas have their own characteristics. Typical of Shakrisabz are strong colours and bold floral motifs together with dark foliage. *Suzani* from Bukhara usually have a lattice design in the central field, while those from Nurata are the most naturalistically drawn and comprise flowering plants placed diagonally to a central star pattern. Common to all the embroideries are the floral motifs themselves and their design influences. Central Asia was at the crossroads of the trade routes from East to West and the interchange of decorative ideas from China to Persia all left their imprint.

1 *Suzani, Shakhrisabz, South Uzbekistan, 19th century.*

2 *Ruidhzo suzani, Bukhara District, 19th century.*

3 *Nimsuzani (small hanging), Bukhara District, 19th century.*

Near Eastern Ceramics

The Near Eastern ceramics in the Collection range in date from the 9th to the 17th centuries A.D. and cover an area from Turkey in the west to Samarkand in the east. From them, it is possible to gain some idea of the variety not only of shapes but of decorative techniques and motifs to be found among products of the Near Eastern potter's art.

The early ceramic wares of this region fall into two basic body types: earthenware and fritware. Earthenware is made from secondary clays of various colours, is nonvitreous and is fired to quite a low temperature. Fritware is a mixture of secondary clays and frit, that is, a silicate that has been melted and then reground. A version of fritware was used by Near Eastern potters to imitate the imported Chinese porcelains that attracted so much admiration. This was so-called soft-paste. Since the feldspathic clays necessary for fine porcelain are virtually nonexistent in the Near East, the potters combined secondary clays and glass frit, including potash, to make a body that was then covered by an alkaline glaze and that could be fired at about 1100 degrees centigrade to produce a vitreous white material. This clay was quite easy to work and could be potted to such a thinness that it was translucent when fired. Two other ways of imitating the white bodies of Chinese wares were also used: one method was to apply a white slip – a sloppy clay-water mixture – to the body before decoration or glazing; the other was to use a so-called tin glaze. This name is slightly misleading since it was still a lead glaze like the others in popular use at the time, but it had added to it tin-oxide particles which were suspended in the glaze to produce an opaque, whitening effect.

Most vessels were made on the potter's wheel, although some shapes and decorative relief effects obviously lent themselves more readily to moulding or modelling techniques. From the information currently available, it seems likely that the pots were fired in an up-draught kiln, that is, one where the heat is drawn up through a perforated floor. For the sake of economy the pots were often stacked one on top of the other, when they were placed in saggers – fire-resistant ceramic boxes – which also protected them from kiln debris, or were separated by using stilts. In the latter case, the marks of the stilts often remain on the fired pots.

It is often very difficult when discussing the ceramics of this large area to say with any certainty where a particular type of pot was made. Early literature on the subject is limited, apart from the Kashan potter Abul-Qasim's treatise of the Muslim year A.H. 700 (A.D. 1301), and too few properly controlled archaeological excavations of kiln sites have been carried out to allow a clear picture to emerge. In addition, the unifying effect of Islam meant that wares travelled easily from one area to another, so finds from archaeological excavations other than at kiln sites can be quite misleading.

Chinese pots imported into the Near East had a considerable effect on its own ceramics. The wares of the Chinese Tang Dynasty (A.D. 618-907) were much admired and imitated: *sancai* multicoloured splashed wares, green-glazed wares and Tang white wares were all copied by Near Eastern potters. In fact, these last – the white wares – began what some scholars see as one of the primary themes of Islamic ceramics: the search for white. Some of the ingenious techniques that the potters of the region employed to overcome the fact that they did not possess the white clays of China have already been described. Other elements of Chinese ceramics were also admired and adopted, as discussed later, but it should certainly not be thought that the potters of the Near East merely copied ideas from elsewhere; they were also very innovative and produced some dramatic and beautiful decorative ideas of their own.

Some of the earliest Near Eastern pots in the Collection are those decorated by painting with the slip mixture in natural colours. These date from the 9th and 10th centuries A.D. and were made in the area of Khurasan ruled by the Tahirids (A.D. 822-872) with their capital at Nishapur, and Transoxiana, both regions being ruled from 874 to 999 by the Samanids who had their capital at Bukhara. In the case of the straight-sided bowl here, a pale slip has been applied over the body to provide a dramatic contrast with the decorative elements peculiar to this ware that have been painted over it in brown, red and yellow. A quite different effect has been achieved on the shallow dish where the geometric slip-painted designs have been highlighted with white dots of slip on the dark lines and brown splashes on the pale leaf-shaped motifs. The designs are covered by a clear glaze, since if the slip is left uncovered it has a tendency to peel away.

A technique known as sgraffito – scratching – has been used to great effect on several Near Eastern wares. Some of the most appealing, of which there are a number of examples in the Collection, are those from the Garrus region of northwestern Persia between the 10th and 13th centuries A.D. The body of the vessel, usually a bowl, is covered with a pale slip, and the design is cut through the slip to leave sections of the dark body exposed in contrast. The contrast was not infrequently heightened by painting the exposed areas of the body with brown pigment. The central medallion of the decoration is usually occupied by a human or animal figure, mythical or real, as is the case in the bowl illustrated here with its human-headed beast. The well is either decorated with a pattern which makes maximum use of the contrast

1 *Bowl, Khurasan or Transoxiana; shallow dish, Persian, Nishapur, 9th-10th century, diameters 25.4cm (10in) and 12.3cm (4⅞in).*

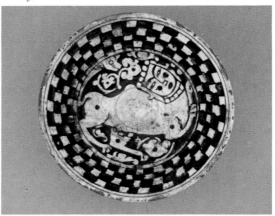

2 *Sgraffito bowl, Persian, Garrus area, 10th-13th century, diameter 16.1cm (6⅜in).*

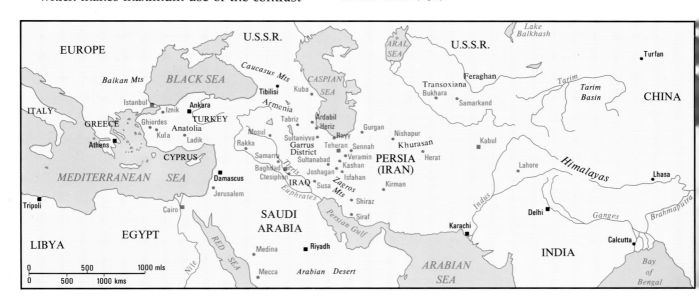

3 Silhouette ware bowls and jug, Persian, 12th-13th century, diameters of bowls 18cm (7⅛in) and 21.2cm (8⅜in), height of jug 12.7cm (5in).

4 Bowl with painted decoration and bowl with pierced design, Persian, 12th-13th century, diameters 20cm (7⅞in) and 17.1cm (6¾in).

effect, as here, or else with scrolling designs or more figures. The vessel is also covered by a clear glaze.

In the 12th and 13th centuries, a variant of the sgraffito technique was produced on a ware probably from northern Persia. This has been called silhouette ware because the decorative effect is achieved by applying a black slip over a pale body and then carving the design through the slip. The vessel was then covered by a clear colourless glaze or, more often, a richer-looking turquoise one, as on the examples in the Collection. The designs fall into two distinct types: geometric designs relying on straight lines and dots, as on the 3 deep bowl and the jug; and beautiful

arabesques, like those inside the shallow 3 bowl, which create what are surely some of the most elegant ceramics to come from the Near East.

4 At first glance the next bowl looks as if the same decorative technique has been employed, but closer inspection reveals that the design has in fact been painted in black onto the pale body before it was covered by a clear turquoise glaze. This technique dates from the late 12th or early 13th centuries A.D. and was perhaps a refinement of the silhouette technique since it allowed freer and more detailed decoration.

Turquoise – which was supposed to ward off the evil eye and whose copper-oxide colouring agent was cheap and easily available, hence its popularity – was also used as a monochrome glaze. In fact, with the importation of the monochrome wares of the Chinese Song Dynasty (A.D. 960-1279) came the determination of the Near Eastern potters to produce a substitute for porcelain. By using the techniques already described (see page 73), plain white wares were made, and also white wares with splashes of colour, as well as pieces with monochrome glazes.

4 The lovely bowl here displays not only an attractive clear turquoise glaze but a beautiful carved scrolling design which, while it no doubt was influenced by the carved designs on Chinese white and celadon wares, is very Near Eastern in execution. This bowl also shows how the malleable soft-paste body could be more thinly potted than its earthenware counterpart; in this case the thinness has been emphasized by piercing the body at various points in the design and filling the holes with glaze to draw attention to its translucent qualities.

Of the monochrome glazes, turquoise, coloured by the addition of copper oxide, dark blue coloured by cobalt, and aubergine coloured by manganese, were the most popular. Turquoise was used not only as a clear glaze; sometimes tin oxide was added to 5 make it opaque, as in the bowl with the band of relief-script decoration. Script of various styles is a common decorative feature of Near Eastern ceramics. Sometimes it is legible, in which case it often provides a quotation from the Koran or a poem, on other occasions it is 5 purely decorative and meaningless. The bowl

5 *Blue bottle, aubergine bowl, turquoise bowl and blue bowl, Persian, 12th-13th century, diameter of blue bowl 18.4cm (7¼in), height of bottle 27.3cm (10¾in).*

6 Lajvardina *jug and* minai *bowl, Persian, 12th-13th century, diameter of bowl 19.6cm (7¾in), height of jug 24.7cm (9¾in).*

with the aubergine glaze has inside the rim a band of decoration which has been produced by simple incising – another decorative technique that was very popular and particularly effective with a deep monochrome glaze. The shape of the deep
5 bowl with the cobalt-blue glaze is one that appears also with turquoise. It is octagonal and has a moulded cartouche on each facet. In this case, the cartouches contain a pair of confronted beasts under a decorative canopy.
5 The cobalt bottle also has a moulded relief decoration, a particularly well-executed version of the popular motif of animals and scrolls.

Contrasting with these single-colour wares, the Collection also has examples of some of the highly decorative Near Eastern polychrome wares. One of these is the ware produced in the 12th and 13th centuries and usually called *minai* ware, from the Persian word for enamel. On this, as many as seven colours were used to produce very detailed decorative motifs, frequently consisting of
6 small figures, as on the bowl here, horsemen,

trees, geometric patterns and arabesques. The basic technique is that of overglaze enamels, where the pot is glazed and fired, then the enamels are applied on top of the glaze, and the pot is fired again at a lower temperature. In addition to these overglaze enamels, however, it is not uncommon to see some underglaze decoration in blue or turquoise and occasionally some overglaze gilding which greatly enhances the richness of the pot's appearance.

Another highly decorative polychrome ware, which may have been made in Kashan, is the so-called *lajvardina* ware. When the *minai* wares went out of production at the time of the Mongol invasion of Persia in the 13th century A.D., they were replaced by *lajvardina* ware which had itself ceased to be made by the end of the 14th century. The name derives from the word *lajvard* which means "lapis lazuli", but because lapis lazuli cannot produce a colouring effect in a glaze, in this case it actually refers to cobalt which does. As **6** can be seen from the jug here, it is a very sumptuous-looking ware, and indeed its relatively short production period could well be explained by its expense – not only overglaze enamels of red and cream but also applied gold leaf make up its rather stiff and formal decorative scheme, not unlike those seen on Near Eastern embroidery and metalwork. It is not surprising to find that pieces were used for official gifts, such as those sent to the vizier Rashid-al-Din by the Sultan of Delhi in 1308.

An entirely different but equally decorative, and indeed short-lived, ware is also of the Il-Khanid – or Mongol – period, more precisely the 14th century. This is the type known as Sultanabad ware, because it has traditionally been presumed to come from that area of central Persia. Sultanabad wares seem to have been influenced by Chinese ceramics, not only in the actual decorative motifs but also in the colour. Perhaps as a result of the influence of the greyish tone of the celadon wares, these Sultanabad pieces have a rather more grey body than those of the previous century and are more heavily potted. In some instances a grey slip has even been used for the ground colour. Another innovation which tends to add to the heavy appearance of this ware is the use of a thick

7 *Sultanabad ware bowl, Persian, 12th-13th century, diameter 16.5cm (6½in).*

white slip to produce decoration in low relief – a technique that can be seen on some tiles in the Collection. But it is in bowls such as the **7** one here that Sultanabad ware can be seen at its most attractive. The characteristic underglaze decoration has not drawn too heavily on Chinese motifs and the painted black outlines have not been deluged but skilfully highlighted by cobalt blue and turquoise.

Perhaps the decorative technique most readily associated with the Near East is, however, lustre. Its origins are still somewhat obscure, but it seems likely that it was invented by the glassmakers of Egypt in the 8th century A.D., about the time of the Islamic conquest, and from there to have spread into Syria, Iraq and Persia. The lustre effect was achieved by glazing, usually in cream but occasionally in blue, firing the pot or tile, then using a mixture of silver and copper oxides, sulphur, red or yellow ochre and vinegar to paint a design on the surface of the opaque glaze. The object was then fired again at a low temperature in a reducing atmosphere which drew the oxygen out of the metal oxides. When the object was cool, the ochre was gently rubbed off to reveal the design as a metallic sheen on the glaze. This metallic sheen is not generally easily damaged, but excessive exposure to the weather or burial in damp conditions can have a disastrous effect. Unfortunately, either of these has frequently been the case with excavated examples from

8 *Lustre bottle and bowl, and lustre and blue bowl, Persian, 12th-13th century, height of bottle 34.9cm (13¾in), diameters of bowls 18.7cm (7⅜in) and 19.6cm (7¾in).*

9 *Lustre star and cross tiles, Persian, late 13th-early 14th century, width of star tiles 31.1cm (12¼in).*

which the sheen has therefore disappeared, leaving the design in plain brown.

The Collection has a number of lustreware 12th and 13th-century pieces in the styles associated with the Rayy and Kashan areas. The lustre on this bowl is particularly well preserved and the richness of the metallic sheen can be fully appreciated. Like the turquoise bowl, this bowl also makes use of script as part of the decoration, but in two different styles. The inscriptions around and just inside the rim are written in a legible cursive script, while the band in the bottom of the bowl is a formal design based on Kufic script. Another bowl also incorporates script in its decoration, this time on the outer rim. On this piece the lustre has been combined with underglaze blue which has been used to highlight the decoration, dividing the segments of the design inside the bowl and emphasizing the edge. The lustreware bottle is a strange but not untypical combination of shaping and decoration. The faces around the mouth pick out the lobed effect rather well, while the framing around the medallions, with their characteristic kneeling figures, is slightly raised above the surface of the rest of the body to give the whole design greater impact.

Fine lustre painting is to be seen on some of the wide variety of tiles in the Collection, particularly the star and cross tiles here. These were made in Kashan in the 13th century and very probably came from a saint's tomb, the Imamzadeh Yahya at Veramin, southeast of Teheran, which was originally decorated with lustre tiles. By the end of the 19th century none of the tiles remained at Veramin, but a good number are to be found in museums around the world. Quite a few of them are dated, and the inscriptions around their edges are all quotations from the Koran.

An equally magnificent tile, although employing a very different technique, is the large twelve-pointed star tile. Probably made about 1400, it has been decorated by the *cuerda seca* technique which first appeared in Persia in the 14th century and which may have been developed as a cheaper substitute for mosaic, making use as it does of the same colours. The beautiful arabesque design is in blue, turquoise, white, red and gold, the last two applied over the glaze. The different glaze colours were prevented from running into each other by a wax and manganese line between them that burned away in the firing to leave only a dark outline.

Despite their ingenuity, the potters of the Near East did on occasion simply copy **11** Chinese examples slavishly, as in the green dish, an example of Near Eastern celadon of the 13th or 14th centuries. Even its decoration has been taken from the Chinese repertory, but whereas the Chinese regarded fish as symbols of fertility and always used them in pairs, the Near Eastern potter has used five. **11** The underglaze-blue bowl dates from the 16th or 17th centuries and has no pretensions at all to be anything but a copy of Chinese ware. The figures are even dressed in Chinese-style clothes and are placed in a Chinese-style landscape complete with pagodas. **11** The large blue and white dish is also a direct copy of a Chinese prototype. It is a mid-16th-century copy of a 15th-century Chinese dish with the shape of the piece and each element of the decoration faithfully repeated, but it does·bring us into the realm of the Turkish potters of Iznik. Iznik wares first

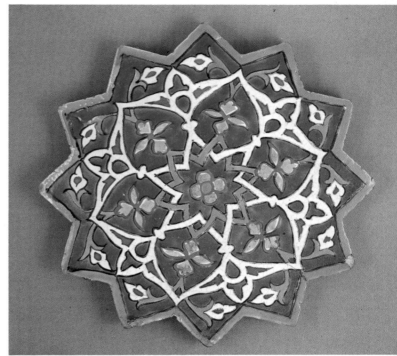

10 Cuerda seca *star tile, Persian, c.1400, width 40.6cm (16in).*

11 *Iznik blue and white dish, Turkish,* c.*1530, diameter 41.9cm (16½in); celadon dish, Persian, 13th-14th century, diameter 32.7cm (12⅞in); blue and white bowl, Persian 17th century, diameter 23.8cm (9⅜in).*

appear to have been made in the 15th century and continued into the 17th century, but nearly all the pieces in the Collection date from the middle period, the 16th century. The decorative elements on these Iznik pieces can be divided fairly easily into Chinese *Hatayi* elements and Turkish or Islamic *Rumi* elements. Bearing in mind the Chinese-style wave design around the rim of this dish, we can see a very much debased version still being used in combination with the more Islamic decoration of S-shaped serrated

12 leaves, tulips and carnations on the next plate,
12 while the tankard restricts itself to Islamic elements. The plate and tankard show the palette and decorative scheme most readily associated with Iznik ware – the body of the ware is soft-paste over which a white slip has been applied. Over the slip the designs have been painted in black outline, blue, green and a bright scarlet then covered by a transparent alkaline glaze. The red pigment which often stands in slight relief on the surface of the vessel is made of a clay called Armenian bole, giving an effect known as sealing-wax red or

13 tomato red. The two jugs use the same palette as the dish and tankard but in a rather

different way. The scale effect in the background may indeed be due to Chinese influence, but the flowers on the one, and more especially the arabesques on the other, are purely Islamic.

12 *Iznik dish and tankard, Turkish,* c.1650-1700, *diameter of dish 28.5cm (11¼in), height of tankard 20.3cm (8in).*

13 *Iznik jugs, Turkish,* c.1650-1700, *heights 27.9cm (11in) and 26.6cm (10½in).*

Near Eastern Carpets

The textiles of the Near East have long been widely admired, to both East and West. Even in medieval Europe, the elaborately decorative fabrics of the Islamic world were in great demand, but it is the carpets and rugs of the Near East that have consistently found favour abroad, and have indeed, in the West, become so much a symbol of luxury that the words 'Persian carpet'' conjure up a picture of elegance and opulence.

It is the pile carpet which has been the most popular, that is, a carpet made by stretching warp threads on a loom and, in addition to weaving weft threads across them as in normal flat-weaving technique, knotting extra pieces of wool, silk or cotton around the warps between the wefts to stand above the surface and form a pile which can later be trimmed to length. Two types of knot, both of which attach to two warp threads, are used in the Near East – the Turkish or Ghiordes symmetrical knot, and the Persian or Sennah assymetrical knot. The names, however, are not a reliable guide to where the carpet was made, as both techniques travelled widely.

It is not at all certain when the first pile carpets and rugs were made, but in the 1940s a Russian excavation of the 5th or 4th-century B.C. tomb of a Scythian chief in the Altai region of Siberia yielded a saddlecloth made of pile carpet, approximately two metres square. Both Babylon and Persia have been put forward as the place of manufacture, but it is more important to note that this is a very fine piece of carpet, with more than 30 knots to the square centimetre, showing that the technique of carpet-making was well established by this early date.

It was at the end of the 11th century A.D., at the beginning of the Crusades, that carpets began to arrive in Europe in considerable numbers, and by the end of the 14th century there was an established carpet stall in Bruges, run by Armenians. From existing inventories, it is known that the monarchs of 16th-century Europe had collections of carpets, although of these only part of the collection of the Austrian house of Hapsburg has survived. Perhaps the most interesting remaining

testament to the popularity of Near Eastern carpets is to be seen in paintings, especially those of Flemish and Italian artists from the end of the 15th century onwards. Indeed, some types of carpet have become rather loosely known as, say, ''Holbein'' or ''Lotto'' carpets, after Hans Holbein and Lorenzo Lotto, in whose paintings they appear.

In Europe, Near Eastern carpets were used on the floor, but often they were also used to cover benches and cupboards and were hung out of windows on festive occasions, as can be seen in the paintings of the late 15th and early 16th-century Venetian artists Carpaccio and Crivelli. In the Near East, carpets were, and have always been, primarily used as decorative floor coverings, but it is worth remembering that there it was customary to remove one's shoes before walking upon them. Moreover, there is less furniture to cover a carpet in a Near Eastern room, and traditionally people sat on the carpet or on

1 *Fragment of a grotesque animal carpet, Indian, late 16th-early 17th century, 266.7 ×269.2cm (105 ×106in).*

cushions or low divans so that they were nearer to the floor and could better appreciate the texture and design of the carpet.

The carpets in the Burrell Collection date from the 16th to 19th centuries and come from a wide range of geographical areas, including Turkey, the Caucasus, Persia, central Asia, and India. Among the carpets from India, a large fragment more than two and a half metres square is of 16th or early 17th-century date and has a particularly fascinating design. Formerly in the Imperial collection in Vienna, it is the largest of several fragments in museums around the world, which come from what must once have been a very large and magnificent carpet featuring a design of flowers and grotesque animals. All kinds of animals and birds – both real and imaginary – are depicted emerging from each other's mouths. The origin of the design is perhaps a strange mythical animal which appears in book illustrations of the same period.

Strange animals and plants are also the theme of another very fine Indian border fragment of the same date, but the treatment is quite different. In the other, the plants are individual sprays whereas here they form a lattice of which the animals are an integral part. The animals and, in this case, fish are not nearly so grotesque; indeed, the horses are handsome animals while the lions are singularly lacking in ferocity. The fabric itself is exceptionally finely made, and although the pile is wool the warps and wefts are of silk, with approximately 77 knots to the square centimetre.

A small but extremely beautiful border fragment comes from what is possibly the most famous of all Persian carpets, the so-called Ardabil carpet. There were, in fact,

3 *Fragment from an Ardabil carpet, Persian, 1539-40, 32.3×20.3cm (12¾×8in).*

2 *Fragment of an animal carpet, Indian, 16th-17th century, 40.6×78.7cm (16×31in).*

4 *The Wagner Garden Carpet, Persian, 17th century, 530.8×431.8cm (209×170in).*

two such carpets in a rather poor state, which were sold by the mosque of Ardabil in the 1880s to raise money for repairs. By using pieces from both, a single beautiful carpet was made which is now in the Victoria and Albert Museum in London. Of the remaining pieces, most were used for a carpet that is now in the Los Angeles County Museum in the United States, while the rest, like the one in the Burrell Collection, survive as fragments in various museums around the world. The carpets are dated by inscription to the Muslim year A.H. 946 (A.D. 1539-40), and were made for the shrine of Sheikh Safi, the founder of the Safavid Dynasty. The inscription, appearing in a cartouche at one end of the carpet, begins with two lines from a poem by Hafiz, and has been translated as:

"I have no refuge in the world other than thy threshold/There is no place of protection for my head other than this door/The work of the slave of the threshold/Maqsud Kashani in the year of 946."

The carpet is very fine, with a woollen pile and wefts but silk warp threads, with a knot count of over 77 to the square centimetre. Like the previous animal fragment, it is very soft and the velvety pile is cut very short. Although it requires more work and is therefore more costly, the more closely knotted a carpet is the shorter the pile may be cut and the more clearly the fine details of the design may be seen, hence the saying, "the thinner the carpet the richer the Persian".

4   Contrasting with this small fragment, another Persian carpet is one of the largest in the Collection, measuring well over five metres by four. This is the famous Wagner Garden Carpet which takes its name from a previous owner. Its date has been the subject of much discussion, but it seems most likely that it was made in the first half of the 17th century. The design portrays a traditional formal Persian garden with a pool, water channels, pathways, trees and flowers, and even the birds, animals and fishes have been included in delightful detail. Living as they did in an area that is so often dry and barren, it is not surprising that the artists of the Near East have found the theme of a luxurious garden an appealing one, and hence it is one that recurs in paintings and in literature. In

5 *Arabesque carpet, Persian, 17th century, 347.9 × 284.4cm (137 × 112in).*

the case of garden carpets, the great precursor was surely the famous carpet made for the Sassanian King Chosroes Nushirvan, which was known as "Chosroes' Spring" but which no longer exists as it was cut up as booty at the fall of the city of Ctesiphon in A.D. 637. That early garden carpet was, however, almost certainly a flat woven carpet rather than one with pile; knotted garden carpets probably did not appear until the 16th century.

The Wagner Garden Carpet is a good example of the way Near Eastern carpets were designed to be enjoyed from close proximity. While the overall decorative scheme is very pleasing, the details provide an almost unending source of delight: the ripples on the water; the ducks swimming upon it or, with wings outstretched, in flight; the timid animals looking fearfully at their predators while the bolder ones venture even onto the pathways to break the strict formality of the garden's layout.

Perhaps the motif that is most readily associated with the Near East, and particularly the arts of Islam, is the arabesque,

6 *Dragon carpet, Caucasian, 17th century, 505.4×243.8cm (199×96in).*

the stylized plant design drawn in graceful curves to form a regular and often complex pattern. Another Persian carpet in the Collection is a beautiful 16th or 17th-century example of the way these arabesque designs were used on early carpets. This is basically a medallion carpet in design, with a border composed of two major arabesques intertwined with a further minor one. The central medallion and the four corner pieces are also formed of arabesques, and the background is a complex interweaving of arabesques and floral motifs.

While arabesques provide the lattice on this last carpet, a very different kind of lattice can be seen in the magnificent dragon carpet from the Caucasus, of 17th-century date. In this case, the motif derives from a serrated-leaf shape and is used to produce a blue diamond lattice overlaying a white one, while more plant and animal forms appear on the lattice itself. At the axes of the lattice, and in some of the cartouches formed by it, are decorative elements derived from leaves, flames and flowers, but it is the animals on this carpet and its antecedents that are the fascinating element, particularly the dragons. The dragon as a decorative theme was introduced to the Near East from China, but its treatment on this carpet owes nothing to the Far East. The dragons here are angular, fashioned in blocks

of colour and in numerous twisting shapes. One has a bird for an eye, another a leaf, while others still are decorated with strings of flowers. This carpet shows the dragon design at its height, for although dragon carpets continued to be produced, the decorative elements became more and more debased, and in later examples are barely recognizable.

A type of rug quite familiar to western observers is the prayer rug. These are usually less than two metres long and can be rolled up and carried about fairly easily. They can be used by devout Moslems to kneel on and face Mecca for the required periods of daily prayer. Today, the floors of mosques in the Islamic world are often covered by these small rugs. The prayer rugs in the Collection come from various regions in Turkey, such as early versions of the type associated with the area around Ghiordes. As well as decorative floral designs, these rugs incorporate, as many prayer rugs do, the architectural feature of the mihrab, the prayer niche in a mosque wall which indicates the direction of Mecca. Some rugs have a basket of flowers hanging in the niche while others have a mosque lamp, which symbolizes eternal light, or a ewer for water, which emphasizes cleanliness. The different rug-making areas each have their own individual styles, several of which can be seen in the Collection.

Medieval Europe

Northern European art of the period *c.*1300-*c.*1500 was always Sir William Burrell's first love, and it is without doubt the strongest part of the Collection, as Burrell himself recognized. It was chiefly with Late Gothic and Early Renaissance art that he surrounded himself in his homes at 8 Great Western Terrace, Glasgow, and Hutton Castle in Berwickshire.

Precisely what aroused Burrell's interest in the Middle Ages is not certain. Possibly he was influenced by the ruins of the Cathedral and Archbishop's Palace at St Andrews, which he knew from his schooldays, or by the medieval castles of the Fife peninsula, with which he was well acquainted. In the late 19th century he was friendly with R. W. McKenzie, the owner of Earlshall Castle, and must have admired the collection of tapestries there. At the end of the 19th century, Burrell even tried to buy the ruins of Newark Castle, near St Monans, with a view to restoring it and living there.

By the beginning of the 20th century Burrell already owned several medieval tapestries, a few medieval sculptures in wood, alabaster and ivory, and a number of bronze and brass domestic utensils, including candlesticks. He also possessed ecclesiastical objects such as an enamelled pyx and a copper-gilt chalice. Stained glass at this point did not figure largely in his interests, but was soon to do so. He continued to add to all these areas almost to the end of his life. Most of the outstanding tapestry acquisitions were made in the late 1920s and 1930s, and his collection of stained glass was raised to the first rank by a series of purchases in the years immediately preceding and following the Second World War. Some of the best items of medieval sculpture were bought in the last ten years of his life. The tapestries were by far the most expensive of the medieval acquisitions, and he was on occasions prepared to pay more for tapestries than he did for paintings (he used to say that you got far more for your money if you bought tapestries).

Burrell's eye for quality and his discerning judgement were, as always, important factors, and he was aided by a group of specialist dealers with good knowledge and sources of supply. The group included John and Gertrude Hunt, from whom Burrell obtained some of his finest sculptures and *objets d'art;* Wilfred Drake, his trusted adviser on stained glass; and Frank Partridge and Frank Surgey, who chiefly sold him furniture and tapestries. A number of the best tapestries and sculptures, however, were acquired from Arnold and Jacques Seligmann and Maurice Stora in Paris. Each of these dealers discovered that even within the confines of the medieval period Burrell had his likes and dislikes. He never cared very much for illuminated manuscripts, nor for anything much earlier than the beginning of the 14th century: it was only with the greatest difficulty that he could be persuaded to purchase 12th-century pieces in the Romanesque style. It is somewhat ironic that some of the most highly valued medieval objects in the entire Collection are Romanesque, including the Temple Pyx and the Prophet Jeremiah stained glass panel.

Sandstone portal from Hornby Castle, English, early 16th century, 6.86 ×2.29m (22½×7½ft).

Sculpture and Church Art

Today the objects produced by the craftsmen of the Middle Ages are viewed for their intrinsic value as art. Contemporaries would have seen them in a rather different light: to them they were chiefly made for the glory of God, in many instances specifically for use in Christian worship. Thus the majority of the medieval items in the Collection, apart from those of a practical or domestic use, have a religious subject or originally had an ecclesiastical context. This applies as much to the monumental carved portals and arches as to the tiny ivories.

The architectural features have been incorporated into the fabric of the Burrell Collection to act as a framework for the smaller items. They were purchased by Burrell in 1953/4 from the Hearst Collection for trifling sums, having for the most part lain in unopened crates ever since the American newspaper magnate had acquired them. Some had even crossed the Atlantic to be built into Hearst's legendary Californian residence at San Simeon and then been returned to the United Kingdom. One that falls into this category is the late 12th-century limestone **1** portal which originally formed the west entrance to the nave of the parish church at Montron, near Château Thierry in eastern France. Although the carved details have been heavily restored, the winged creatures set amongst coiling foliage on the capitals are typical examples of the world of monsters and strange beasts created by Romanesque sculptors. Such frivolities within a monastic context attracted the wrath of St Bernard of Clairvaux who was afraid that monks would be dangerously distracted: "We are more tempted to read in the marble than in our books". His strictures are easily applicable to the Montron portal: "What profit is there in those ridiculous monsters, in that marvellous and deformed comeliness, that comely deformity?"

The exuberance of the Montron portal may be contrasted with the restrained decoration of the three windows placed on the Mezzanine overlooking the Tapestry Gallery, and of the doorway in the South Gallery outside the Hutton Castle Dining Room. These four items date from the early 13th century and originally formed part of a house in Provence. Their hard limestone enabled the southern French carvers to achieve great precision in the carved details, the capitals and the spiralling columns. The doorway with its pointed arch also has a slightly Islamic flavour, explained by its original geographical proximity to Spain, at that time still largely under Moorish control and influence.

Also from a domestic rather than an ecclesiastical context is the largest of all the built-in architectural features. This is the elaborate portal giving access from the Courtyard into the North Gallery, which is illustrated on page 86. With the 14th/15th-century doorway forming the principal entrance to the building, it comes from Hornby Castle in Yorkshire. This castle dates from the 14th century but was, in the words of the early 16th-century antiquary John Leland, "but a mean thing" until "William Conyers, the first lord of that name . . . did great cost on Hornby Castle". William, Lord Conyers (1468-1524), fought at the Battle of Flodden in 1513 and was Constable of Richmond and Middleham Castles. His refurbishments at Hornby included this portal which bears the name "Conyers" on the arch and the family arms quartered with various alliances between supporters. The lavish heraldic display is typical of many Early Tudor monumental entrances, and the Hornby Castle Portal is paralleled by a number of contemporary gateways to Oxford and Cambridge colleges. The two shields to the left of the niche containing the lion are earlier in date than the portal and are not *in situ*. The early 13th-century carvings of the woman carrying a pitcher and the bird-like creature are also not part of this doorway but are located on each side in approximately the same position they occupied at Hornby Castle. The oak door with its tracery, decorative carvings and iron studding is original.

In the late Middle Ages heraldry was by no means confined to architectural features but is

1 *Limestone portal from Montron, French, late 12th century, 4.72×3.81m (15½×12½ft).*

2 *The Bury Chest, English,* c.*1340, painted oak, length 194.3cm (76½in).*

3 *Detail from painted limestone tomb, Spanish, mid-14th century, length 157cm (62in).*

found proclaiming ownership and association on all manner of objects. The Bury Chest is one of a very small group of English oak coffers with painted heraldic decoration. It bears the arms of Richard de Bury, Bishop of Durham (1334-45), and of Ralph, 2nd Lord Neville (d.1367), who was overseer of the temporalities of the See of Durham during the bishop's absences. The royal arms of England quartering France almost certainly refer to Richard de Bury's services to the English crown, which included acting as Lord Treasurer and then Lord Chancellor for brief periods. The bishop, who was also lay ruler of the Palatinate of Durham, was noted for his splendid retinue and sumptuous living. During the Scottish wars he placed all the shipping of the Palatinate at Edward III's disposal for transporting troops and, at his own expense, provided twenty men-at-arms and twenty archers. Neville spent most of his life fighting the Scots and is remembered especially for his victory at the Battle of Neville's Cross in 1346, when King David of Scotland was taken prisoner. The Chest was, until the mid-19th century, in the Court of Chancery of the Palatinate of Durham and was probably used to contain documents.

3   The tomb placed near the Bury Chest dates from the same period, but comes from much farther south. The effigy represents a Spanish knight of the Espés family, said to be Don Ramon Peralta de Espés (d.1348), Captain-General of the armies of the Kingdom of Aragon and Grand-Admiral of Aragon and Sicily. He enjoyed a reputation for valour, on one occasion fighting in his own galley with only sixty knights against seventeen galleys of the enemy. In style and design and in the emphasis on the fine details of dress and accoutrements, the tomb is closely related to a group of sepulchral monuments to the Counts of Urgel from the monastery of Santa María de Bellpuig de las Avellanas in Catalonia in northern Spain, which is now in the Cloisters museum in New York. The Espés tomb, which retains much of its original painted decoration, was originally in the monastery of Santa María de Obarra at Calvera, near Huesca, also in northern Spain. The curious foreshortening of the effigy can be explained by its original location in a narrow niche.

There are few examples of Spanish

4 *Painted wood figures of St John and the Virgin, Spanish, late 13th century, height 122cm (48in).*

5 *Ivory mirror case, French, early 14th century, diameter 8.2cm (3¼in).*
6 *Painted limestone standing figure, French, c.1250-75, height 86cm (33¾in).*

7 *Boxwood Virgin and Child, French, c.1325-50, height 33.6cm (13¼in).*
8 *Marble female saint, German, early 14th century, height 28cm (11in).*

medieval sculpture in British galleries so the Burrell Collection is fortunate in also
4 possessing two polychromed wood figures of the Virgin and St John from a large Crucifixion group of the late 13th century. The triangular drapery folds of the St John and the contorted stance of the Virgin show the introduction of French High Gothic forms into the local Romanesque tradition.

There are altogether more than 300 medieval carvings in wood, stone, alabaster

and ivory in the Collection, ranging in size from nearly life-size figures down to small ivory carvings such as the early 14th-century
5 French mirror case depicting a couple playing chess. The sculptures fall into two basic groupings: individual devotional figures, and those which originally formed part of retables, or altarpieces. Within the former category it is possible to study the main stylistic developments in northern Europe between the late 13th and the early 16th centuries; in addition there are some earlier pieces.

The grace and sensitivity which characterize late 13th-century sculpture were first evolved by the artists of Paris and eastern France around 1230 to 1240. The limestone
6 standing figure, probably of an angel, shows why French sculpture was admired and imitated throughout Europe. The broad drapery folds, the slightly swaying posture and the idealized face combine to give a gracious and serene impression. The figure dates from the third quarter of the 13th century and is similar to a series of stone angels formerly in the church of Notre Dame at Poissy and now in the Louvre, Paris.

The stylistic characteristics established by the French sculptors of the middle decades of the 13th century were retained for the next 150 years, as is demonstrated by the boxwood
7 Virgin and Child. The affinities with the limestone angel are so striking, especially in the heads, that we might be pardoned for supposing that the two are not far apart in date. In fact, the boxwood statuette belongs to a later group of sculptures carved in Lorraine in eastern France around 1325 to 1350. The chief difference lies in the more decorative treatment of the Virgin's drapery, with the folds falling in multiple cascades.

A manneristic trend becomes apparent in sculpture during the last years of the 13th and the early 14th centuries, with full-length figures taking a pronounced S-shape and *contraposto* stance, and with the limbs and torso completely hidden by swathes of drapery. This treatment of figures was not confined to France but spread throughout northern Europe. A small marble female saint
8 shows the North German version of this style and is related to the figures on the high altar of Cologne Cathedral. The style is found in both monumental and miniature sculpture, such as

9 the ivory diptych with scenes of the Nativity, the Adoration of the Magi, the Crucifixion and the Coronation of the Virgin. The diptych was carved in northeastern France, or possibly even the Liège area of the Low Countries. The exaggerated poses, particularly of the swooning Virgin and of Christ in the Crucifixion scene, suggest a date of *c.*1360 to 1370.

The 1370s and 1380s witnessed a movement away from the mannered elegance of earlier
10 years. The alabaster group of the Holy Trinity is one of the finest English carvings of the period *c.*1375 to 1385, and in its impression of volume and solidity is far removed from the ethereal qualities displayed by the sculptures previously discussed. It bears a strong affinity to contemporary manuscript illuminations, such as the *Lytlington Missal* of 1383/4.

From the second half of the 14th century alabaster, quarried in Nottinghamshire, Derbyshire and Staffordshire, became a major medium in English sculpture, being used for devotional images, tombs and altarpieces. The technical skills of the English alabaster carvers were on the whole not high (the Holy Trinity group being one of the few exceptions), and their work relied heavily for effect on the polychromed and gilded decoration. Their counterparts in France, Germany and the Netherlands were much more proficient in the use of this material, particularly the anonymous artist known as the Master of Rimini after a Crucifixion group in a church near Rimini in Italy. The nationality of the sculptor has not been established, but between *c.*1420 and 1430 he seems to have settled in the Middle Rhine area
12 of Germany. The Pietà group in the Burrell Collection is unlikely to be by the Rimini Master himself but is more probably a late work from his atelier, dating from *c.*1430 to 1450. The complex and deep drapery folds create a sophisticated play of light and shade.

The dominant sculptural form of the 15th and early 16th centuries was the altarpiece, or retable. The retable was an object directly responsive to the needs of devotion: it proclaimed the identity of the saint or subject to which the altar was consecrated; it glorified the Eucharist which was daily renewed upon it; and it gave the individual sculptures a stage from which to exercise the image's duty of

9 *Ivory diptych, French or Netherlandish, c.1360-70, 14.5×18.5cm (5⅜×7⅜in) open.*

10 *Painted alabaster group of the Holy Trinity, English, c.1375-85, 88.9×33cm (35×13in).*

narrating and impressing. The precise form retables took varied even within countries. The most elaborate and attractive were the

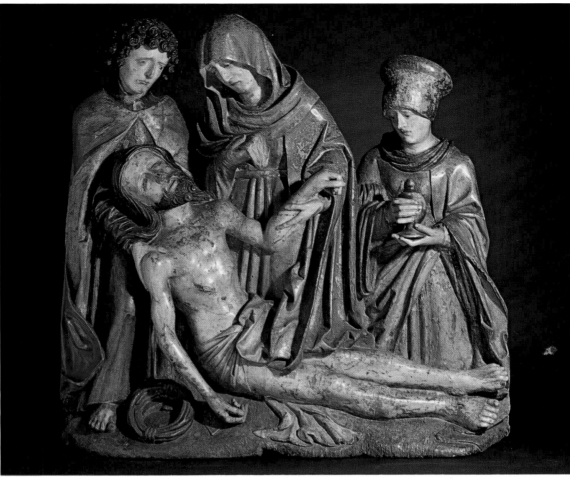

11 *Painted limewood Lamentation over the crucified Christ, German, c.1510-20, 109.2×106.7cm (43×42in).*

12 *Alabaster Pietà, German?, c.1430-50, length 30.5cm (12in).*

limewood altarpieces of southern Germany and those from the Tyrol, which were made of pine. The late 15th-century altarpiece from these regions consists of a *corpus* in the centre, containing a single scene or row of saints; wings, either painted on both faces or painted on the exterior and carved in low relief on the interior; and a *predella,* placed under the *corpus* in order to raise it sufficiently to allow the wings to be closed or opened. The fourth component is the elaborate openwork traceried superstructure above the *corpus,* often containing saints or angels. There is no complete southern German or Austrian retable in the Burrell Collection, but it does include a number of sculptures from altarpieces from these regions. The **11** polychromed limewood Lamentation over the dead Christ almost certainly belonged to a *corpus.* It dates from *c.*1510 to 1520 and is related in style to the work of the Augsburg

13 *Painted pine angel figures with lute and organ, Austrian, c.1490-1500, height 55.8cm (22in).*

15 *Painted and gilded oak angel figures with shields, German, c.1500, height 54.1cm (21½in).*

14 *Limewood Nativity, German, c.1500, 66×66cm (26×26in).*

16 *Oak St Barbara, Netherlandish, c.1520, height 56.5cm (22¼in).*

13 carver Loy Hering. The two angels playing musical instruments come from the superstructure of a Tyrolean retable of *c.*1490 to 1500 and can be attributed to Hans Klocker, a leading Late Gothic sculptor of the region.

Until the 1490s, retable sculpture was invariably polychromed, giving an illusion of movement and a hallucinatory effect perfectly suited to their religious function. Retables continued to be polychromed after the 1490s but in Germany an alternative appeared in the form of the monochrome, or unpainted, altarpiece. The first known South German unpolychromed retable was made in 1490/2 by the famous Franconian sculptor Tilman Riemenschneider for the town church at Münnerstadt. This was an important innovation. The abandonment of the gesso sizing for taking the paint enabled sculptors to carve very fine details. The difference in surface effect is demonstrated by a comparison of the polychromed Lamentation **14** with the monochrome low-relief Nativity from the wing of a Franconian retable dating from *c.*1500. Like so many southern German sculptures of the period, the composition of the Nativity is based on an engraving by Martin Schongauer.

The limewood used for the Nativity relief is a hard wood and is good for carving because of its tractability. It readily yields across the grain and is soft to work. On the other hand, it is liable to crack owing to uneven shrinkage or drying. One of the means the southern German sculptors adopted to circumvent splitting was to carve in thin membrane-like forms and avoid inherently unstable solid masses. These thin structures were particularly suitable for rendering drapery, as the Nativity demonstrates. This feature distinguishes the limewood sculptors from their northern German and Netherlandish counterparts working in oak. Oak is less easy to carve than limewood but does not crack so readily. The first factor effectively prevented virtuoso carving in the limewood manner and, together with the second, resulted in the retention of large solid masses, as shown by the pair of polychromed **15** angels which are almost certainly the work of the Cologne sculptor, Tilman van der Burch, **16** active around 1500; and also by the figure of St Barbara, carved in *c.*1520 by a craftsman

from the Maastricht area. The emphasis on the accoutrements is typical of Netherlandish sculpture of the period. The St Barbara is a single devotional image and does not come from a retable.

Altarpieces were produced in large numbers in the southern Netherlandish cities of Brussels, Antwerp and Malines. So standardized was the formula, both in the design of the retables and in the details of carving, that it is difficult to distinguish the work of one centre from another. The Malines carvers also made a speciality of lavishly gilded and polychromed statuettes of female **17** saints, like the attractive Virgin and Child. On the Virgin's drapery is the letter M, the mark of the Malines guild of sculptors.

17 *Painted and gilded oak group of the Virgin and Child, Netherlandish, c.1500, height 37.4cm (14¾in).*

Another small-scale object of which Netherlandish craftsmen seem to have made a speciality was the cradle-reliquary containing a figure of the Christ Child. These became popular as devotional images from the 14th century onwards, and were frequently **18** found in convents. The example in the Burrell Collection dates from the late 15th century and retains its gilding and polychromy. The Child is missing, but the cradle still has miniature figures of St Martin and the Pietà.

19 Alabaster group of the Virgin and Child, Netherlandish, late 15th century, height 36.8cm (14½in).

18 Painted and gilded oak cradle, Netherlandish, c.1480-1500, height 25.4cm (10in), length 19cm (7½in).

Most Netherlandish carvers worked in oak or walnut, but limestone and alabaster were also used. A very fine piece in alabaster is the **19** half-length figure of the Virgin holding the Child, dating from the last quarter of the 15th century (the metal crown is of recent date). It is reminiscent of contemporary Flemish paintings, a resemblance which must have been even more striking when it had all its gilding and painting.

As mentioned earlier, alabaster is a prominent feature of English late medieval carving. Apart from individual cult images like the Holy Trinity, most sculptures in this medium were made for altarpieces which were very different from the wooden retables produced in Europe, and consisted of a row of panels enclosed within a wooden framework. The quality of the carving is never very sophisticated but, as the Adoration of the **20** Magi panel shows, the application of gilding

20 Alabaster panel of the Adoration of the Magi, English, late 15th century, 40.6×25.4cm (16×10in).

21 *Marble bust of a boy, Italian, c.1480, height 24.1cm (9½in).*

and polychromy to the monochrome alabaster can be very effective. This relief is displayed amongst a series of panels which come from various dismembered altarpieces.

It is a far cry from the world of the English late 15th-century alabaster carver to that of his Italian Renaissance contemporary. On the whole, Burrell did not care for art from south of the Alps, but his few forays in that direction sometimes reaped rich rewards, such as the **21** marble bust of a boy, possibly the work of the Florentine sculptor Benedetto da Maiano (1422-1497). It forms a fitting companion to the *Virgin and Child* by Giovanni Bellini which is illustrated and discussed on page 139, in the chapter on paintings.

So far, sculpture has been discussed only in terms of individual devotional images or altarpieces, but it was also employed on more utilitarian church furnishings, especially seating. English late medieval craftsmen made a speciality of decorative and figural carving on bench-ends and misericords, those hinged seats which form part of church stalls; when the seat was tipped up, a projecting ledge on the under side provided a support for the clergy during lengthy services. These ledges allowed the sculptor to give full rein to his imagination, and all manner of subjects were represented, no means all of them strictly religious and frequently of a droll **22** nature. The misericord illustrated here is one of the more restrained, showing the Ark containing Noah and his wife and various beasts.

22 *Oak misericord depicting Noah's Ark, English, 15th-early 16th century, height 29.8cm (11¾in), length 59.6cm (23½in).*

23 *Oak desk-end depicting St Quirinus, German, late 15th-early 16th century, 122×30.5cm (48×12in).*

24 *Detail from orphreys on Italian dalmatic, English, late 14th century, 35×17cm (13¾×6¾in).*

Commissions for church stalls would not always go to journeymen craftsmen but sometimes to sculptors of distinction. **23** The oak desk-end carved with the figure of St Quirinus of Neuss is closely related to the work of the Lower Rhenish sculptor Heinrich Bernts (d.1509).

The occupants of the stalls were the clergy, passively or actively involved in what was the central function of the Church, the celebration of the Mass. The liturgy, that is the formal rites and services of the Church, and the sacred objects used in its performance during the Middle Ages were created not for their beauty alone but for the greater glory of God. It was upon them that the richest materials and most skilled craftsmanship were lavished. This applied as much to the vestments worn by the officiating clergy as to the sacred vessels. English medieval embroidery was famed throughout Europe, and especially in the 13th and 14th centuries it was sought after by the greatest potentates, including popes and cardinals. The Burrell Collection has an Italian dalmatic – a tunic worn by deacons at Mass –

24 with two wide strips of English embroidery featuring scenes from the early life of the Virgin. These orphreys, as the strips are known, date from the late 14th century when *opus anglicanum* was past its prime, but the dalmatic is particularly important as it forms part of a set of vestments said to have been made for the Cistercian abbey of Whalley in Lancashire. The rest are at Townley Hall, Burnley, and together they form the only complete pre-Reformation set of English High Mass vestments, apart from a 16th-century set in Oxford.

The vessel central to the Mass is the chalice, and appropriately they were made of precious metals and often richly embellished with

25 jewels and enamels. The silver chalice illustrated here is partly gilded and has translucent enamels on the knop. On the base are the embossed figures of the donors, George and Margaret Sperling, kneeling before the Virgin and Child. It was made in northern Germany in the late 14th or early 15th centuries.

Bronze ewers in the form of real or fantastic creatures were used for the liturgical ceremony of the washing of the priest's hands during Mass. They are known as *aquamaniles* (from the Latin *aqua* meaning "water" and *manus*, "hand"), and there are several in the

27 Burrell Collection. This one is in the shape of a lion and dates from the first half of the 14th century. That aquamaniles were not just confined to Christian liturgical use is shown by the Hebrew inscriptions on this piece and its provenance: it comes from a synagogue at Brilon in Westphalia, Germany.

During the Middle Ages, relics of Christ's Passion and of the Virgin and the saints were scattered throughout Western Christendom. To contain these relics, a wide variety of shrines or reliquaries was created. Very few from the medieval period have survived, especially in England where in the 16th century the Reformation took an almost complete toll of such objects. Because of this,

25 *Silver chalice, partly gilt with traces of enamelling, German, late 14th-early 15th century, height 16.4cm (6½in).*
26 *The Temple Pyx, English or German, 12th century, bronze-gilt, 9.2×7.3cm (3⅝×2⅞in).*

27 *Bronze aquamanile, German, c.1300-50, 29.8×33cm (11¾×13in).*

26 the bronze group of three sleeping soldiers, almost certainly representing part of a Holy Sepulchre scene, takes on an added significance. The piece is known as the Temple Pyx as it is reputed to have been found in the Temple Church in London. Several similar pieces are recorded, and it seems likely that they all originally formed part of a reliquary or shrine. If the provenance is correct, the Temple Pyx may well be English, although it is usually considered to be German. It dates from *c.*1125 to 1150.

29 A much more complete reliquary *châsse,* or casket, also has an English connection although it was made in France. The copper-gilt and *champlevé* enamelled box has a scene of the murder of Thomas à Becket, the premier saint of England, to whose shrine at Canterbury pilgrims flocked from all over Europe. This *châsse,* which in the 18th century belonged to the celebrated collector Horace Walpole, was made in Limoges at the beginning of the 13th century. In the 12th and 13th centuries the city of Limoges specialized in the production of enamelled and copper-gilt objects, not only *châsses* but also many other liturgical items such as crosses, basins, candlesticks and covers for service books. The

30 cover shown here, depicting the Crucifixion in low relief, dates from *c.*1195.

During the 14th and 15th centuries, there developed for private use a devotional book known as the Book of Hours. This was an abbreviated version of the service books used by the clergy, like the Breviary and the Missal, and, as its title suggests, it included prayers and readings arranged according to the eight canonical hours of the day. Books of Hours were frequently lavishly illuminated and highly prized. Some of the finest are French.

28 The Collection has one which was written and decorated for a Breton lady around the middle of the 15th century, with additional text and illustrations added later in the same century. Amongst the original miniatures in it is the Annunciation to the Shepherds at the beginning of the hour of terce.

29 *Enamelled* **châsse,** *French, c.1200-10, 17.2×12cm (6¾×4¾in).*

28 *Pages from* Book of Hours of the Virgin, *French, 15th century. 18.4×12.7cm (7¼×5in).*

30 *Enamelled Crucifixion plaque, French, c.1195, 16.5×11.2cm (6½×4⅜in).*

Tapestries

Sir William Burrell, with justification, regarded his tapestries as the most valuable part of his Collection. There are more than 150 examples, most of which date from the late 15th and early 16th centuries, representing all the major centres of production.

Tapestries were woven for use as altar frontals and as wall-hangings in churches as well as private houses. They were also regularly hung in the streets during great festivities, and the powerful ecclesiastical and secular princes took them from one residence to another and even on military campaigns. Tapestries were tangible signs of the rank and wealth of a prince, and enormous collections were acquired by the great potentates. Philip the Bold, Duke of Burgundy, at his death in 1404 owned no fewer than seventy-five. A century later, those two great rivals Henry VIII of England and Francis I, King of France, had large numbers; the latter had more than two hundred tapestries in his stores of furnishings in Paris.

The princes of France and the Netherlands also found tapestries a valuable bargaining counter in diplomatic negotiations with rulers lacking an indigenous tapestry-weaving craft. In 1411 and 1416 John the Fearless, Duke of Burgundy, sought to ally himself with England by gifts of tapestries. This sumptuous art was also coveted beyond the confines of Christendom. One measure adopted by Philip the Bold to alleviate the effects of the disastrous defeat of a Crusade at Nicopolis in 1396 was to offer tapestries to the victorious Turkish Sultan Bayezit.

The subjects represented on medieval tapestries cover a wide range. Scenes from the Old and New Testaments are common, as are allegorical themes and those based on mythology and romance. Pastoral scenes of the hunt and themes of the Labours of the Months were popular on tapestries woven for private houses, as opposed to churches. Heraldry also figures prominently, and there are purely decorative subjects.

Tapestries were much used for the decoration of churches in Romanesque and even earlier times, but survivals from anywhere prior to the 14th century are few and far between. Even 14th-century tapestries are scarce, although the activities of weavers based in Arras and Paris are recorded from the early years of that century. The Burrell Collection is fortunate in possessing several examples from this epoch. The earliest is a
1 fragment showing interlaced lozenges filled alternately with monsters and pairs of birds. It is part of the furnishings from an altar and dates from about 1300. There is an identical piece in the museum at Freiburg-im-Breisgau in southern Germany, which is said to have come from the Dominican convent of Adelhausen near that city. Both fragments were almost certainly woven in that region.
2 The set of three armorial hangings displayed in the Hutton Castle Hall and Drawing Room formed part of a very large series of which other portions survive in the Metropolitan Museum, New York, the Rijksmuseum in Amsterdam and other

1 *Tapestry fragment with birds and monsters, German, c.1300, 54.5×50.8cm (21½×20in).*

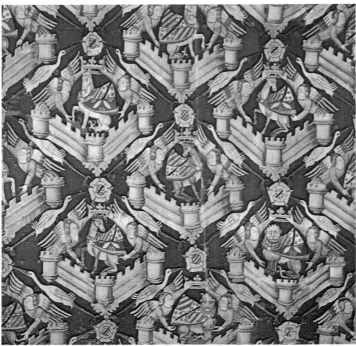

2 *Beaufort-Turenne-Comminges armorial tapestry, French, late 14th century, 221×216cm (87×85in).*

3 *Angel, possibly from the Angers* Apocalypse *series, French, c.1375-1400, 91.4×83.8cm (36×33in).*

collections. The hangings have the arms of Beaufort, Turenne and Comminges occurring variously on lions, stags, elephants and unicorns framed by battlements and angels; filling the spaces between the enclosures are storks and rosettes, the latter bearing alternately the arms of Beaufort and Turenne. The set was almost certainly commissioned by William III of Beaufort, who married Eleanor of Comminges in 1349, and by his only son Raymond, created Vicômte de Turenne in 1375. Both men held key positions in the papal state at Avignon during the pontificate of William's brother Gregory XI, and the hangings were probably woven in Paris between 1375 and the pope's death in 1378.

William of Beaufort subsequently entered the service of that great patron of the arts, John, Duke of Berry. On 7 April 1377, the Duke's brother, Louis I, Duke of Anjou, paid 1,000 francs to Nicholas Bataille "for the making of two cloths of tapestry of the Story of the Apocalypse which he did for the Duke" This referred to the famous *Apocalypse* tapestries, now displayed in the château at Angers. The set is not quite complete, and it is generally considered that two fragments in **3** the Burrell Collection, one of which is shown here, originally belonged to it; at the very least, they were assuredly woven in the same workshop. The precise role of Bataille in the Angers *Apocalypse* series is disputed, but it seems that he was a Parisian merchant who owned tapestry workshops rather than a weaver himself. The cartoons, or designs for the series, were the work of the French King Charles V's court painter, John of Bruges, and underline the close relationship between the various arts that existed in the Middle Ages.

From the 15th century there survive many tapestries from France, the Netherlands and the German-speaking lands, including Alsace and Strasbourg. Unlike that of the Netherlands, German tapestry weaving never became a highly organized commercial industry, but seems to have been carried out in small workshops in convents and houses. The products are small in size in comparison with the works of their counterparts farther north. Their weavers were only modestly accomplished, but the appeal of the tapestries lies in the naivety and almost childlike simplicity of the designs. A favourite source of subject matter was the wild men who were believed to inhabit fields and forests. Such creatures (or ordinary people dressed as wild **4** folk) appear in an early 15th-century tapestry in company with peasants engaged in hay-making. Below the harvesters are sprites riding hobbyhorses, picking flowers and playing musical instruments. The hanging personifies the month of July and probably formed part of a set illustrating the Labours of the Months. The inscriptions on the scrolls are in a German dialect with certain peculiarities which point to an Alsace origin for the tapestry.

From the same area, but dated to the last quarter of the 15th century, is the small **5** tapestry depicting Fidelity in the form of a stag being driven by hounds and a couple mounted on horseback across a flower-strewn meadow towards a net slung between trees. The words on the scroll indicate that the lovers are hunting Fidelity, than which nothing dearer can be found. The tapestry is

5 The Pursuit of Fidelity, *German, c.1475-1500, 76.2 ×86.4cm (30 ×34in).*

4 The Month of July, *German, c.1400-25, 94.6 ×152.4cm (37¼ ×60in).*

6 The Adoration of the Magi and St Erasmus and St Dorothy, *German, c.1471-80, 91.4 ×198cm (36 ×78in)*.

noteworthy for the excellence of the drawing and the fresh observation of nature.

The market for these tapestries was chiefly to be found amongst the ranks of the wealthy patrician families of the German cities, just as they were the main donors of painted and carved altarpieces. The design of the altar **6** frontal representing the Adoration of the Magi is, in fact, based on the format of a retable, with two saints separated from the main scene by vertical lines, as if they were on the wings. The saints are the patrons of the Schurstab family which commissioned the tapestry and is shown kneeling in prayer. Erasmus Schurstab is on the extreme left and his first wife, Dorothea Hallerin, on the right. Between them are their seven sons and six daughters, together with Schurstab's second wife, Ursula Pfinzing. The eldest daughter is dressed as a nun, and the frontal was probably woven for, and perhaps in, her convent of the Holy Sepulchre in the city of Bamberg, north of Nuremberg. It can be dated to between 1471 and 1480.

7 The Bible Tapestry is the largest German hanging in the Collection. It was woven in the Middle Rhine in the early 16th century and comprises thirty-four Old Testament and two New Testament scenes, representing a synopsis of the history of mankind up to the birth of Christ. The overcrowded arrangement, with the small, puppet-like figures, is of considerable effect but a far cry from the sophisticated products of the contemporary weavers of the Low Countries.

During the 15th and early 16th centuries, the Dukes of Burgundy and their Hapsburg successors actively encouraged weaving in the Netherlands to replace the cloth manufacture which had suffered severely from English competition. These rulers and the members of their courts commissioned large numbers of tapestries both for themselves and as gifts, and Flemish tapestries were greatly prized throughout Europe. It was a highly organized industry, very different from the domestic pastime enjoyed by nuns and secular ladies in Germany.

It is a difficult task to assign individual works to a particular town or city since there were looms in all the major urban centres of the Netherlands, and the weavers moved freely among them. One instance may suffice to warn of the dangers of over-simplification in attributing tapestries: an Arras citizen named Baldwin of Bailleul designed a tapestry of the Golden Fleece for Duke Philip the Good (d.1467) from preliminary sketches done in Bruges; the tapestry itself was woven in Tournai.

A number of works have, however, been convincingly attributed to Tournai. Through the large-scale patronage of Duke Philip and his son Charles the Bold (d.1477), this city supplanted Arras as the leading centre of production around the middle of the 15th century. The principal workshop there in the third quarter of the century was controlled by Pasquier Grenier, although, like Nicholas

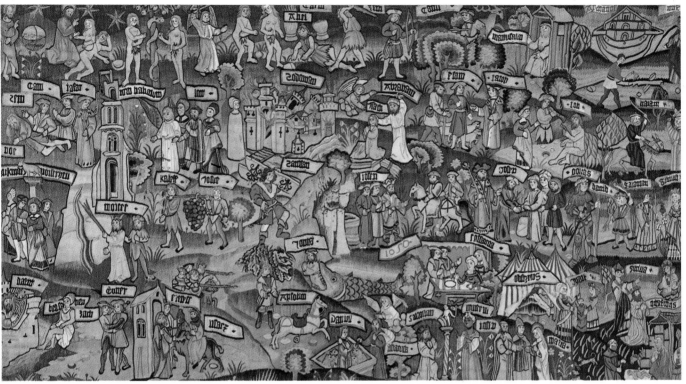

7 Bible Tapestry, *German, early 16th century, 149.8×271.8cm (59×107in).*

Bataille, his precise role may have been more
8 entrepreneur than weaver. *Peasants Hunting
Rabbits with Ferrets* is perhaps a product of
Grenier's looms. It is certainly one of the finest
tapestries of the period, displaying a sense of
movement and naturalism together with an
interest in perspective. The tapestry shows
the preparatory stages of the rabbit hunt –
sharpening a peg, taking a ferret from its
basket, laying nets over the rabbit holes, and
restraining the dogs on the leash. The
beautifully delineated rabbits at the base of the
tapestry appear unperturbed by all these
activities. Two more hangings from the same
set, in San Francisco and the Louvre in Paris,
depict the hunt itself and the subsequent
picnic.

The other end of the social spectrum from
the country folk engaging in their rural
9 pursuits is shown in *Hercules Initiating the
Olympic Games*. Here, the Burgundian court
appears in all its magnificence under the thin
disguise of mythology. The Dukes of
Burgundy claimed Hercules as an ancestor
and admired him as a model of courage and
physical prowess. The mounted figure of
Hercules bears a strong resemblance to
portraits of Philip the Good, and the young

8 Peasants Hunting Rabbits with Ferrets, *Franco-
Burgundian, c.1450-75, 304.8×292.1cm (120×115in).*

105

9 Hercules Initiating the Olympic Games, *Franco-Burgundian,* c.1450-75, 386×477.5cm (152×188in).

man to the left may be intended to represent his son and successor, Charles the Bold. The tapestry may have been a ducal commission to commemorate the latter's first joust which took place in 1451.

12 The upper border of hanging bells to *The Camp of the Gypsies* is a characteristic feature of tapestries attributed to the workshop of the early 16th-century Tournai weaver Arnoult Poissonnier. His inventory mentions a large number of hangings entitled "The Story of Carrabara, so-called of the Egyptians", that is, gypsies. The series to which this tapestry originally belonged may have been inspired by a visit made in 1421 by gypsies to Tournai. In the foreground a young man is having his fortune told whilst the attention of a companion is diverted from a stolen purse

being concealed in a bowl of fruit. Amongst the scenes of music-making and amorous dalliance, the gypsy mothers feed and nurse their babies.

10 The large tapestry known as *The Camel Caravan* may also have been based on an historical event. The Portuguese explorer Vasco da Gama's voyages to the East Indies in 1497/9 and 1502/3 aroused much interest, and in 1502 a procession of exotic beasts through the streets of Antwerp was organized by the Portuguese. It is just such a cavalcade which is depicted in this hanging, with Indians riding the camels and engaged in peddling. Their humble attire contrasts dramatically with the rich clothing of the Portuguese. Intermingled with the camels are lions and monkeys. The tapestry is one of a group of about fifteen

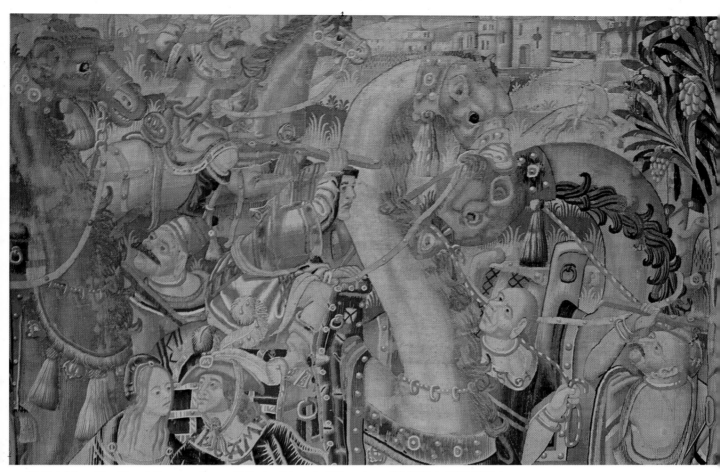

10 *Detail from* The Camel Caravan, *Franco-Netherlandish, early 16th century, 360×649cm (142×255in).*

11 *Detail from* The Flight of the Heron, *Franco-Netherlandish, early 16th century, 318.7×309.8cm (126×122in).*

12 *Detail from* The Camp of the Gypsies, *Franco-Netherlandish, early 16th century, 386×343cm (152×135in).*

13 *Detail from* Charity Overcoming Envy, *Franco-Netherlandish, late 15th century, 247.6×213.3cm (98×84in).*

with the same theme, which can be associated with the workshops of Pasquier Grenier's sons, John and Anthony, and of Arnoult Poissonnier. In their inventories, the tapestries are described as "in the manner of Portugal and India", "the story of Calcou", and other titles.

11 The huntsmen in *The Flight of the Heron* tapestry are placed in a setting complete with peasant houses and a castle, a landscape reminiscent of the illustrations done a century earlier by the Limbourg brothers for the famous manuscript known as the *Très Riches Heures.* The combat between hawk and heron, which according to a later 16th-century treatise on falconry was esteemed the noblest flight of all, is portrayed with a remarkable degree of realism. The principal huntsman, mounted on a richly caparisoned white horse, may represent the French king, Francis I; if so,

the tapestry may be based on one of a lost set of hangings depicting the hunts of this monarch.

One of the most debated questions in the history of tapestry is where the very attractive tapestries known as *millefleurs* were woven. These are so called from the placing of figures against a background entirely filled with flowers. Many bear the arms of nobles who lived in the magnificent châteaux which adorn the river Loire where the French court was frequently in residence. This has led some authorities to suggest that an important workshop was settled there, or that itinerant weavers came to the area for specific commissions. More recently, it has been shown from documentary evidence that *millefleurs* tapestries (or *verdures* as they were called at the time) were woven in Brussels. The matter remains open, for there are certain

14 *Detail from* The Arms of Miro, *Franco-Netherlandish, early 16th century, 353×330.2cm (139×130in).*

15 *Detail from the Luttrell Table Carpet, English or Netherlandish, mid-16th century, 193×551cm (76×217in).*

technical arguments against all *millefleurs* tapestries having been woven in Brussels, and almost all of the finest examples have a French provenance.

13 In the highest category is *Charity Overcoming Envy,* which is displayed in the Hutton Castle Drawing Room. It was purchased by Burrell at the beginning of this century and hung in his Glasgow home, prior to his acquisition of Hutton Castle. Against a dark-blue background strewn with clusters of flowering plants, Charity, in the guise of an elegantly attired lady mounted on an elephant, raises her sword to strike the cowering figure of Envy, riding on a dog. The Latin text above can be translated to read: "The wretchedness of an envious mind is next to a bag of onions, rejoicing in his evil like a dog, but this elephant ignores evil and brotherly charity crushes it." This tapestry almost certainly formed part of a long set depicting a series of battles between the Seven Cardinal Virtues and the Vices mounted on allegorical animals. The combat between virtues and vices was a popular theme in medieval iconography.

14 The tapestry with the arms of the Miro family shows a development of the *millefleurs* ground into a more naturalistic landscape setting. The shield bearing the mirror device, a punning reference to the name of the patron, Gabriel Miro, is suspended from the principal tree. Miro was a member of a distinguished family of royal physicians and became doctor-in-ordinary to the French king, Louis XII (d.1514), and subsequently to his daughter Claude, queen to Francis I. The robes of the angels and the humanistic script of the motto in the border proclaim the infiltration of the Italian Renaissance into the art of the tapestry weavers of the north.

So far, only wall-hangings or altar frontals have been considered. The last illustration is **15** of a tapestry designed for neither of these locations but for use as a table carpet. The central field comprises an interlocking complex of squares, circles and quatrefoils enclosing various flowers and three shields of arms; twelve more armorial devices occur in the border. The arms are those of Sir Andrew Luttrell of Dunster in Somerset and his wife, Margaret Wyndham. The marriage took place in 1514 when they were both minors. Sir Andrew died in 1538, and the tapestry may

have been commissioned by his widow. In her will, dated 9 March 1580, she bequeathed "my best and longest carpett" to her daughter Margaret Edgecumbe, in the possession of whose descendants it remained for centuries. There is only one other 16th-century tapestry-woven table carpet still in existence, now in the Metropolitan Museum of Art, New York. The Luttrell table carpet was probably woven in the Netherlands, although an English origin is also a possibility.

Stained Glass

One of the most colourful aspects of the Middle Ages is the stained glass that filled the windows of churches and, latterly, private residences. Although the craft is known as stained glass, a more accurate term would be painted glass, for the technique consists of painting designs on to coloured and white sheets of glass, which have already been cut to the required shape, and then firing them in a kiln. The glass is subsequently leaded and placed in position.

There are more than 600 panels of stained glass in the Burrell Collection, ranging from complete windows down to small roundels. The Collection is particularly strong in northern European glass of the 15th and early 16th centuries, although there are some important panels of both earlier and later date. Burrell owned ancient glass from quite early in his collecting career and had some important figural panels and armorial glass installed in the windows of Hutton Castle. His most important acquisitions were made in the years immediately preceding and following the Second World War and included some very fine windows purchased from William Randolph Hearst's collection and several extensive series of English 16th-century heraldic glass, which raised this part of the Collection to the first rank.

Clear window glass was known in northern Europe from Roman times, but although there are some fragments of windows with figural decoration dating from as early as the late 9th century, it is only from the 12th century that elaborately decorated glazing survives in any quantities. One of the most important schemes of this period was that commissioned between 1140 and 1145 by Abbot Suger for the abbey of St Denis, just outside Paris. Suger was one of the most outstanding statesmen of the age and well deserved the title of "father of his country", given to him by Louis VII. He is chiefly remembered today for his patronage of the arts, for no single man effected greater artistic changes in the 12th century. His rebuilding of the west front and choir of St Denis marked the beginning of the Gothic style, but in his account of the work Suger was

1 The Prophet Jeremiah, *French* c.1140-1145, 61×33cm (24×13in).

much more concerned with the metalwork and stained glass windows. Little of the glazing survives *in situ* at St Denis, and even today the widely scattered remains are still

2 St Stephen, *German, c.1400, 78.1×35.6cm (30¾×14in).*

1 being identified. One of them is the panel depicting the Prophet Jeremiah, which Burrell acquired in Paris in 1923. Despite Suger's innovations in sculpture and architecture, this figure still retains the hieratic pose and abstract drapery folds characteristic of the Romanesque period. The predominant colours are red and blue, and these remained strong elements in English and French glass until the late 13th century, from which time white glass and more delicate colours played an ever-increasing role. In Germany, the taste for heavy colours persisted much longer, even in non-figural windows such as the attractive ornamental **3** panels with tracery designs and flowers from the former Augustinian church at Erfurt; these date from the first half of the 14th century.

3 *Details from ornamental panels from Erfurt, German, first half 14th century, 91.4×57.4cm (36×23in).*

Strong colours can still be found in German **2** glass of the following century, as in the panel depicting St Stephen, dating from *c.*1400. This also comes from southern Germany, perhaps even from Erfurt, and the elegant pose and heavy swathes of drapery make it a fine example of the International Gothic Style, as interpreted by glass-painters.

The former Carmelite church at Boppard on the Rhine was glazed around 1440. Its windows are now widely dispersed, with the most important divided between the Cloisters museum in New York and the Burrell Collection. In the latter are a three-light window with scenes of the life of Christ and the Virgin; two large figures, of St Cunibert and a canonized bishop; a panel with

4 The Ninth Commandment, *German, c.1440-50,*
114×74.9cm (45×29½in).

5 Solomon and the Queen of Sheba, *German, late 15th*
century, 55.9×50.8cm (22×20in).

the donors of a window, Siegfried von
Gelnhausen and his wife; and part of a
4 Ten Commandments window. The panel
here represents the Ninth Commandment:
on the left is a group of figures bearing false
witness, encouraged by a small flying devil.

Towards the end of the 15th century, the
glass-painters of the Rhineland, in common
with the sculptors, began to copy and adapt
the designs made by the engravers of the
area, such as the Master ES and Martin
Schongauer. The *Solomon and the Queen of*
5 *Sheba* panel is the work of a Cologne glazier
and shows a strong debt to engravings. The
shields to the left of the king bear merchants'
marks and are held by the wild men and
women who appear so often in German Late
Gothic art.

The southern Netherlands, that is the area
roughly contiguous with modern Belgium,
was particularly active in glass-painting
during the late 15th and early 16th centuries.
Through the vicissitudes of history most of the
glass has been destroyed or dispersed so that

even the original location of many of the
surviving windows is unknown. One
6 exception is the panel depicting St Nicholas
saving three men from execution, which was
part of a series of windows commissioned for
the Charterhouse at Louvain by Nicholas
Ruterius, Bishop of Arras (d.1509), an
influential diplomat and important patron of
the arts. Other panels from the same cycle can
be seen in the Metropolitan Museum of Art
in New York and the Victoria and Albert
Museum in London.

The "pictorial" style of glass-painting
evolved in the southern Netherlands during
this period, with its realistic portraiture, use of
landscape and convincing perspective, was
disseminated throughout neighbouring
countries by itinerant Flemish glaziers and
imitated by indigenous artists. One of the
most important of the peripatetic craftsmen
was Arnoult of Nijmuegen (1470-1540) who
established himself at Rouen in Normandy
and, with his pupils, was responsible for
glazing in a number of churches in that city.

6 St Nicholas Preventing an Execution, *Netherlandish, 1509-35, 69.8×49.5cm (27½×19½in).*

7 Princess Cecily, *English,* c.1485, 39.4×29.8cm *(15½×11¾in).*

In England, Flemish glaziers gained a virtual monopoly of all the major commissions during Henry VIII's reign, which is not surprising when the windows of King's College Chapel, Cambridge are compared with work by native craftsmen. These foreign artists had begun to make an impact even before the end of the 15th century, as is demonstrated by the panel depicting

7 Princess Cecily, a daughter of Edward IV. Painted around 1485, it comes from the "Royal" window in the northwest transept of Canterbury Cathedral. Almost certainly a royal commission, it is the work of an accomplished glass-painter strongly influenced by Flemish art.

Throughout the Middle Ages, stained glass was expensive and was considered a luxury art. Consequently, it was found mostly in churches, which were the chief recipients of patronage. As the Middle Ages drew to a close, the wealthier echelons of society increasingly introduced glazing into their houses. Heraldic devices played a major role in domestic glazing schemes, proudly proclaiming the ancestry and connections of the owner. Two of the most extensive series to survive are those from Fawsley Hall in Northamptonshire, the residence of the Knightley family, and Vale Royal in Cheshire. They date from the first half of the 16th century and can be seen in the Restaurant.

9 The medallion illustrated on page 114 encloses the arms of Sir William Brereton, High Sheriff of Cheshire in 1548 and 1552.

Visual puns on the name of the patron also

10 occur. Among the most literal is the quarry, a diamond-shaped panel, showing a man about

9 *Vale Royal medallion, English, mid-16th century,
42.5×31cm (16¾×12¼in).*

10 *Rebus of Abbot Islip of Westminster, English, early 16th
century, 30.5×24.1cm (12×9½in).*

to fall from a tree, together with an eye and
the word SLIP. The device of John Islip, Abbot
of Westminster (d. 1532), it comes from his
chantry chapel in Westminster Abbey.

Roundels depicting the Labours of the
Months became fashionable features in the
windows of private houses in northern
Europe in the same period. Some of the most
attractive are to be found in Flemish and
11 English glass, such as the roundel for
February, illustrating a man warming himself
in front of a fire. This was almost certainly
part of a set which was formerly in the old
parsonage of St Michael-at-Coslany in
Norwich (three others are in the Victoria and
Albert Museum). Norwich was an important
centre of glass-painting in the 15th and 16th
centuries, with several workshops active in
the city. The style of the East Anglian glaziers
is easily distinguishable from glass painted
elsewhere in England, and the roundel is a
characteristic example of their work. Such
vignettes of everyday life remained popular
in domestic glazing well beyond the Middle
Ages, particularly in Holland, Switzerland
and Germany. A roundel depicting the Dutch
tile-maker, Roemt Roomen, engaged in his
craft, shows that such compositions lost none
of their appeal in later centuries.

11 *Labour of the Month roundel: February, English, late
15th century, diameter 23.5cm (9¼in).*

Lace

Lace was a luxury fabric made for over 400 years in many countries, its quality and the technical skills necessary for its production were appreciated by collectors, among them Sir William Burrell. Although the hundred and twenty pieces he acquired range from early 17th century Italian needle lace to 19th century machine-made samples they form only a minor part of his collection as a whole.

Among several interesting pieces in the Collection is a small length of Point de Dieppe Flemish lace from Ghent, depicting the young Charles II of Spain who became king aged four in 1665. This is an example of point lace made in small sections joined together by means of a lace ground. The simple square mesh is an early form in bobbin lace.

The most outstanding item is a length of Point de France, late 17th century, with an allegorical subject of figures, musical instruments, a crown and a bird in a nest whose meaning is unclear. This may be from a set of furnishing lace for use on a dressing table or bed. Other pieces from this or another similar set are in museums in Amsterdam, Cleveland, Washington, New York and Boston. The French needle lace industry was promoted by the government in the late 17th century to provide an alternative to the popular but very expensive Venetian needle lace. Strict control of both production and design ensured delicate lace of the very highest quality.

1 **Punto in aria** *lace, early 17th century, Italian, 15×86cm (6×34in) above.*

2 **Point de France** *lace, late 17th century, 46×117cm (18×46in) right.*

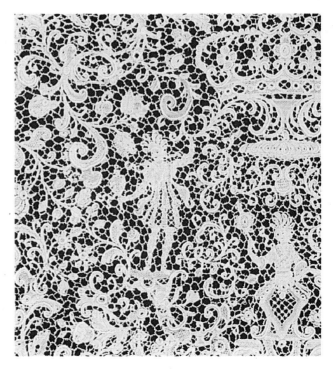

Domestic Arts

During the late Middle Ages, standards of comfort gradually increased in the residences of the upper and middle echelons of society. Glass rather than wooden shutters appeared in windows, walls were covered with panelling and tapestries, and furniture and domestic utensils increased in number and refinement. The most reliable impressions we have of northern European domestic interiors are provided by the paintings of the great Netherlandish artists of the 15th century, such as Van Eyck, Rogier van der Weyden and Hans Memling. Some of the furniture and objects which appear in such paintings, and which could have been found in a wealthy northern European merchant's house of the time, are displayed within an architectural framework provided by panelling from **2** Ipswich and an oak ceiling from a house at Bridgwater in Somerset. The carved bosses and decoration of this ceiling include a Tudor rose surmounted by a crown, which suggests a date in the reign of Henry VII or the early part of that of Henry VIII. Although the ceiling appears to have been constructed for a church (it was installed in the Bridgwater house only in the 18th century), it closely resembles ceilings in houses like that of Thomas Paycocke at Great Coggeshall in Essex, of *c.*1500. The Bridgwater Ceiling may not have an authentically domestic provenance, but there is no doubt about the linenfold panelling. It comes from a medieval merchant's home in Fore Street, Ipswich, which subsequently became a public house under the sign of the "Neptune Inn". The panelling can be dated to *c.*1530 by the Early Renaissance carved frieze above the linenfold.

Of approximately the same date as the Neptune Inn panelling is the oak buffet, or sideboard, bearing the arms and initials of John Wynne of Gwydyr Castle in Wales. The buffet took on an increasing importance in the late Middle Ages as a symbol of estate or honour because of its use for the display of the owner's plate. The buffet's presence indicated that the owner was sufficiently wealthy to have plate worthy of display.

In any such display, a prominent place

1 *Drinking horn with silver-gilt mounts, German, late 15th century, 26.7×27.9cm (10½×11in).*

would have been allotted to the late **1** 15th-century drinking horn from northern Germany. The silver-gilt mounts include finely detailed figures of wild men. Mazer bowls would also have been placed on an English buffet. Mazers were the most popular drinking vessels of the 14th to early 16th centuries. Made of maplewood, they have silver-gilt mounts and a circular medallion in the bottom of the inside of the bowl, which is known as a print or boss. This usually has an enamelled religious device or saint, or the shield of arms of the owner. The medallion in **3** this mazer bears the arms of the Somery and Kippen families.

Heraldic devices representing the owner's status were by no means confined to plate and furniture but also occur in the tapestries that decorated private houses. One, depicting King David and Bathsheba, was woven in the Upper Rhineland in the late 15th century for a Strasbourg merchant, Heinrich Ingold, and his wife Clara.

Religious themes were ever-present even in domestic surroundings. Several of the Nuremberg brass plates on display have embossed Old Testament scenes. In addition, private houses often contained small altarpieces for private devotions. In England,

2 *Oak ceiling from Bridgwater in Somerset, English, late 15th-early 16th century, 5.49×6.1m (18×20ft).*

3 *Maplewood mazer bowl, English, c.1500, diameter 15cm (5⅞in).*

these quite often took the form of an alabaster
4 panel with the head of St John the Baptist on a
charger, surrounded by the figures of saints.
The panel was enclosed within a wooden
box with painted leaves which open out to
form a triptych. Such panels are frequently
mentioned in wills and inventories.

4 *Painted and gilded alabaster head of St John in painted oak box, English, 15th century, 42.6×54cm (16¾×21½in).*

Decorative Arts

Sir William Burrell collected widely and sometimes randomly in the field of decorative arts. It is clear that his first love was for British arts, particularly from the 16th and 17th centuries. The 16th century was the time when Renaissance ideas on form and subject infiltrated into British art, at first intermingling with Gothic forms and soon developing distinctive national features. The elaborate decoration seen on the furniture, silver and needlework of this period indicates that the Elizabethan age was one of newly found wealth – rich in ornament and extravagant ideas. Although British-made items predominate in the Collection, there is a variety of other European wares. Burrell acquired numerous German brass dishes of the 16th century as well as a large quantity of Hispano-Moresque tin-glazed earthenware whose bold sense of design and vitality of execution he found appealing.

The 17th century was a period of constant change, creative energy and experimentation. At first, the reign of James VI and I saw the development of the artistic tradition of the Elizabethan period, but plain, simple designs were preferred around the middle of the century, with the Puritan period of the Commonwealth.

Following the Restoration of the monarchy in 1660, the arts were again lavishly patronized and a great artistic revolution took place. The feeling for beauty of form was to be found, from the most sophisticated of silverware to the charmingly bold slipware of rural potteries. The luxury-loving Charles II, whose taste had been formed in France and Holland, encouraged the trend amongst many of his richer subjects to support and develop the arts. This was also an age of inquiry, not only in the sciences but in manufacturing processes. New methods were devised to improve existing materials, and in particular, towards the end of the century, glassmaking was transformed by George Ravenscroft's invention of lead crystal glass. The Collection has examples of this type of early glass and its subsequent development, in the form of stemmed drinking glasses.

The beginning of the 18th century saw a marked reaction in the decorative arts. Glasses with simple shapes and absence of decoration reflected a wider change where ornament became subordinate to form. In furniture, this change of style can be seen in the splendid bureau cabinet in one of the period rooms, whose appeal is based on its finely figured walnut wood and good proportions. Contemporary silver achieved its effect by beauty of outline, skilfully enhanced by mouldings and faceting. After Queen Anne's death in 1714, a new style succeeded, based on French models. Lighter and more elegant shapes came to the fore, as can be seen again in glasses with their delicate twist stems. Burrell had little interest in either the paintings or decorative arts of this period, so it is paradoxical that he should have bought some outstanding English porcelain figurines that epitomize the carefree rococo manner of the mid-18th century, including the Chelsea Isabella d'Andreini, of which only two other examples are known.

When enjoying these objects, it should be remembered that Burrell bought many of them for his own family use and for the decoration of his homes, not solely as items for display in a museum.

A selection of objects from the Decorative Arts section of The Burrell Collection

Silver

For the last 800 years, the greatest quantity of British silver has been made in London, although there are long-standing traditions of craftsmanship in other parts of the country, with Edinburgh, Norwich, Exeter, Chester and York and many other towns local centres of silversmithing. Gaps in our knowledge of the history of silver have been caused by the very value of the metal. Since 1328, English law has required that wrought silver should be made of sterling silver. This meant, and still means, that sterling silver has only 7.5 per cent copper alloy to 92.5 per cent silver. Since this was the same percentage established for silver coinage, owners of silver not infrequently converted their wares into cash. The dissolution of the monasteries and the appropriation of many Church valuables by Henry VIII also led to the melting down of almost all medieval silver and gold. Other serious losses were caused by the Civil War, when both the Royalists and Parliamentarians raised funds by a levy on silver plate. Despite these events, some medieval silver still exists and much can be learned about its dates and authorship as well as the silver of later centuries from the practice of hallmarking.

By the middle of the 16th century, hallmarks consisted of four distinct symbols: a place mark, the maker's mark, a date letter and the lion passant. The marking system began in 1300 when a statute was passed ordering the wardens of the London silversmiths to mark all plate with a leopard's head before it left their hands, to signify that the piece had been assayed in London and was of the required purity. Other towns were eventually required to have their own marks. In 1363, another law was passed which required all gold and silver to have a unique mark so that the maker could be traced if there were ever a question over the quality of the piece. A date letter, giving the precise year an object had been tested, was introduced by the smiths themselves in 1478, with the letters running in cycles of twenty from then to the present day. The fourth mark, a lion passant, was introduced in 1544, probably as an extra precaution to maintain the sterling quality of

silver, and since 1720 has been used as an assay standard mark in Britain.

The accession of Elizabeth I in 1558 marked an auspicious period for the arts and crafts. As in the Middle Ages, the Church continued to be an important patron of the silversmith because, according to canon law, only silver and gold vessels could be used for liturgical purposes. This resulted in a steady stream of commissions for objects like communion cups, replacing the chalices of pre-Reformation times. Many were quite plain,

1 as this example made in London in 1564/5 shows. The band of decoration, known as flat-chasing, was a peculiarly English method of pattern-making, made by hammering a blunt tool along the lines of the design in a series of small, stuttering advances. The motif of floral scrolls banded by strapwork derives from a Renaissance design.

1 *Communion cup, London, 1564/5, height 14.5cm (5⅝in).*
2 *Tigerware jug, Exeter, 1585, height 24.7cm (9¾in).*

As prosperity at home grew, more people were able to patronize the silversmith. An increasing number of domestic items were made of silver, or at least partly so.

2 The tigerware jug, made in Exeter in 1585, is so called because of the mottled appearance of the earthenware.

While the influences on the design styles of English silver throughout the Tudor and

Stuart periods might derive from Europe, certain types of ware were a specifically English development, such as these 3 magnificent gilded steeple cups of 1611/12. Gilding involved dissolving mercury in molten gold and applying the amalgam to the finished vessels. The cups would then be heated to vaporize the mercury. The term "steeple cup" derives from the finials of their covers, in the form of a three-sided pierced pyramid.

The ornate and richly decorated style of the late Elizabethan period and the early 17th century came to a halt with Puritanism and the Commonwealth. A period of political and economic uncertainty had preceded the years of Civil War, and reaction to this, together with the Puritan ethic of beauty in simplicity and a dislike of any unnecessary emphasis on decoration, made the years of the republic (1649-60) lean ones for the silversmith, with a virtual standstill in the development of new styles. The Restoration of the monarchy under Charles II in 1660 brought an upsurge of demand for silver and silver-gilt. A coconut 4 cup, dated 1662, celebrates his return by recalling how, after the battle of Worcester in 1651, he made his escape from the Parliamentary army by hiding in an oak tree.

The great quantity of domestic silver that had been melted down by both sides during the Civil War had to be replaced. Exuberant designs and large proportions became common until the end of the century. There are even records of silver beds, large mirror frames, tables and chairs being made. Tankards were made to hold as much as three 5 or four pints. These two examples were made twenty years apart, in 1669/70 and 1691/2, but there was little change in design over this period. Their plain bodies are sometimes relieved by an engraved coat of arms, flat cap covers or generous scroll handles.

One of the most far-reaching changes in design development in Britain came with the influx of numerous Huguenot silversmiths after the revocation of the Edict of Nantes by Louis XIV in 1685. For some years before this, less and less toleration had been shown to Protestants in France, and many of them had fled to England to avoid persecution, to the consternation of the British silversmiths who resented the competition. The Huguenots

3 *Steeple cups, London, 1611/12, height of tallest cup 49cm (19¼in).*

4 *Coconut cup, English, 1662, height 19cm (7½in).*
5 *Tankards, London, 1669/70 and 1691/2, heights 15.2cm (6in) and 18cm (7in).*

brought with them an extremely high standard of meticulous finish and new methods of decoration, which were quickly taken up by the English smiths. In particular, the Huguenots introduced a new type of decoration, known as cut-card work, and also

6 *Engraved salver, London,* c.*1695, diameter 34.8cm (13¾in).*

7 *Chocolate pot, London, 1705/6, height 25.5cm (10in).*

raised the art of engraving to unprecedented heights. The chief feature of this splendid
6 salver is the engraved decoration. Within a gadrooned border of ornamental moulding the upper surface is engraved with two medallions, representing both sides of the Exchequer Seal of William III and Mary, on a mantling which also bears the arms of Charles Montagu, Earl of Halifax. Unfortunately, its date letter is indecipherable, but it was made around 1695. This salver represents the custom whereby the holders of certain offices of state were entitled to melt down their official seal for conversion into plate whenever the death of a sovereign made the seal obsolete. When Mary II died on 27 December 1694, the Chancellor of the Exchequer, Charles Montagu, took advantage of this privilege. The artist who carried out the engraving was a Huguenot, Simon Gribelin. In the British Library there is an album of his designs which include this salver, and such was his success with this work that he was awarded the engraving of the next two Exchequer Seal salvers.

The spreading foot and narrow stem of the salver are attached to its underside by cut-card work. This technique can be more clearly seen
7 on the chocolate pot of 1705/6, made by an English smith, Robert Cooper, which has a

sheet of decorated silver applied around the base of the spout. As the term "cut-card" implies, the design is cut from a flat sheet of silver and soldered on to the body of the pot. It was a type of decoration which required a high degree of control and skill, and remained popular well into the 18th century.

The chocolate pot demonstrates how the Restoration ushered in not only an era of extravagance at Court but also many new social customs, such as the growing taste for new drinks introduced from overseas – tea, coffee and chocolate. New silverware forms were quickly devised to hold them. The usual shape for chocolate and coffee pots was a tall tapered cylinder with a wooden scroll handle and curved spout at right angles to the handle. Chocolate was taken strong and thick as the cocoa butter was not removed, so a hole was included in the lid for the insertion of a stirrer.

The next discernible stylistic change occurred while Queen Anne was on the throne (1702-14). Her brief reign has given its name to a whole style of English decorative art, characterised by great simplicity, which lasted for more than a decade after her death. Pieces from this time tend to be simple, practical and symmetrical since ornamentation would raise the prices of silverware still higher.

Arms and Armour

The arms and armour in the Collection include European items from the 13th to the 17th centuries, and the quality of the pieces is generally high. A fine German helmet, known as a sallet, of about 1480 bears the mark of the Augsburg Armourer's Guild. An Italian armet, a type of close helmet designed to protect the head and face, is thought to come from Chester Cathedral. Other helmets of the 16th century, as well as breast and back plates of the following century, are also displayed.

1 An example of a complete armour is the magnificent, fluted German field armour dating from c.1520. It is referred to as "Maximilian" in style, and is made of polished

steel. The surface of the various parts – the helmet, collar, breastplate, arm defences and gauntlets – show a characteristic fluting which was peculiar to German workmanship and originated during the reign of the Emperor Maximilian (1493-1519). Other pieces of armour of the 16th century are decorated with very fine etching, that on the composite three-quarter armour made at Innsbruck being particularly noteworthy.

2 A range of sword types is represented in the Collection. One of the earliest is a two-handed sword of plain cruciform shape, dating from c.1200-50. It is possibly Italian, its iron blade inlaid with latten (a mixed yellow metal similar to brass). Later examples in steel of these large two-handed swords were made in Germany and England. Another weapon used at close range was the mace, and the Collection has a number of Italian, German and French manufacture, dating from the 15th and 16th centuries. Arms with the blade mounted on a long pole include halberds, partisans, glaives, spears and spadroons. Often these weapons were carried by the personal guard of a prince or monarch and were decorated with the ruler's devices and

3 initials, such as this spear made in 1558 for the guard of Ferdinand I shortly before he became Holy Roman Emperor.

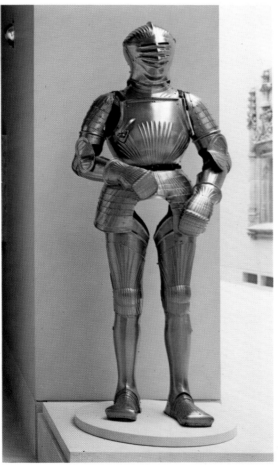

1 *Field armour, German, c.1520-30, height 175.2cm (69in).*

2 *Sword, Italian?, c.1200-50, length 106.6cm (42in).*
3 *Spear, Austrian, 1558, height 215.9cm (85in).*

123

European Ceramics

Sir William Burrell did not set out to collect representative examples of the history of European ceramics. Rather, he selected a few areas and acquired superlative pieces from them. Especially noteworthy are the examples of Hispano-Moresque ware and English slipware.

Hispano-Moresque is the name loosely applied to the lustreware first made in Spain by potters using techniques developed under Islamic rule. After the end of Moorish rule in Andalusia in 1487, the main production of
2 lustreware moved to Valencia where the dish with the Christian monogram IHS was made.
1 Another dish, which dates from the first half of the 16th century, was also made in Valencia which became the centre of Spanish pottery manufacture. Here, the stag, freely drawn in incised blue lines, boldly occupies the whole area of the dish, over an abstract lustred ground. The lustre effect was achieved by applying an oxide of silver and copper which reduced to a film of metal during firing. This type of pottery, with its warm colours and metallic sheens imitating the patina of precious metals, was the finest available in Europe for a hundred years. It is additionally important in that it influenced pottery styles in Italy, to which country it was exported in great quantities from the middle of the 15th century.

The term "maiolica" was applied originally to those lustrewares which reached Italy by way of Majorca, but was extended to cover all varieties of Italian tin-glazed earthernware, as
3 in this early 16th-century dish from a district near Florence, probably Caffaggiolo, where some of the most beautiful Italian maiolica was produced. From the 1470s, the potteries around Florence had developed a rich range of colours to apply to their pieces so they concentrated on the decoration of pottery rather than devising more interesting shapes. The finer pieces generally feature figure-painting rather than purely floral designs, with their subjects taken from the paintings, sculptures and engravings being executed in Florence at the time.

An outstanding place in English ceramic history is occupied by 17th-century slipware, particularly that known broadly as Toft ware. The decoration of pottery by the use of a semi-liquid clay, known as slip, had been in common use in Europe since Roman times. In England, slipware was probably the occasional work of peasant potters who would ordinarily make everyday crockery or roof tiles. The vitality and freedom of design used in the decoration of this branch of earthenware make it noteworthy. The principal centres of production were Wrotham in Kent and, especially, North Staffordshire which was probably the home of Thomas Toft, the most renowned of a family
4 of potters. The example illustrated here, which bears Toft's name, shows a pelican feeding her young with her own blood. The dish is of red clay covered by a yellow slip to provide a light background. A reddish-brown slip was then applied for the design and accented by lines of light-coloured dots. A criss-cross pattern of two different coloured clays was trailed around the rim of the dish, giving an effect not unlike the icing on a cake.

1 *Gold-lustred dish, Spanish, c.1500-1550, diameter 47.6cm (18¾in).*

Polite society came to demand a greater refinement in ceramics which earthenware could not provide, and turned to porcelain. Porcelain had been made in China since the 7th century, but it was not until the 18th century that a comparable material was available in Europe. True hard-paste porcelain was translucent and could be worked to a fine degree, but the secret of its manufacture eluded English factories which devised an artificial porcelain, known as soft-paste. Although it was unable to match the grace of real porcelain, it proved a satisfactory substitute and a suitable material for that lightness of taste known as rococo. Generally, Burrell had little admiration for rococo, but he did own a small but choice group of English porcelain figurines, including the outstanding Isabella d'Andreini, of which there are only two other examples known. This figure was made at Chelsea, the foremost English porcelain factory in England, between 1749 and 1752, some ten years after the factory had been founded. It represents a 16th-century Italian actress famed for her beauty and intelligence, and was modelled by Joseph Willem who dominated figure designs in the early years of the Chelsea works.

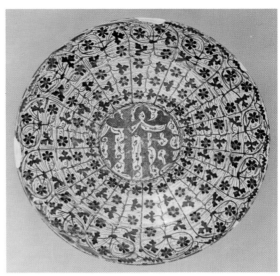

2 *Tin-glazed earthenware dish, Spanish, 15th century, diameter 44.5cm (17½in).*

3 *Maiolica dish, Italian, 16th century, diameter 27.9cm (11in).*

5 *Isabella d'Andreini, English, 1749-52, height 24.1cm (9½in).*

4 *Earthenware dish, English, c.1670, diameter 49.5cm (19½in).*

Treen

The word "treen" means "made of wood", and until the 18th century most simple household articles were wooden. The development of glass and ceramic production, however, gradually phased out the use of wood for the manufacture of domestic utensils. Many of the pieces of treen in the Collection were acquired by Burrell from the collector Owen Evan-Thomas.

While the first requirement of treen was that it should be functional, beauty of form and love of craftsmanship were instinctively present. Suitable timber was carefully chosen so that the desired shape, colour and grain were achieved. There was very little affectation in woodworking, since it was mostly a peasant art and therefore a natural and unconscious form of expression.

The range of forms for general domestic use included trenchers, platters, dishes, bowls and other tableware. The greatest variety is to be found in wooden drinking vessels, and as communal drinking was a feature of many festivities, large-scale cups were required. Vessels for liquids had to be cut from suitable woods, capable of resisting the stresses resulting from alternate wetting and drying. With the introduction from abroad in the late 16th and early 17th centuries of woods more easily worked than the native hard woods, it was possible for the turner to produce suitable large bowls and cups.

Two outstanding examples of treen ware in the Burrell Collection are in the category of standing cups and are based on designs
1 borrowed from silver shapes. The first dates from Elizabethan times and was used for the making and drinking of posset, a concoction of hot milk curdled with ale or wine and often flavoured with spices. The cup, which is turned from sycamore, is decorated with bands of sunk relief, and is made up of several compartments fitting one above the other. Contained within the base are ten roundels of cedar of Lebanon. The upper·section of the base is hollow for holding a lemon, and when inverted it provides a stand for the stoneware pot in which the posset was heated. Above the base is a double cup: the lower inverted one

1 *Standing cups, English: Elizabethan cup, c.1550-1560, height 45.7cm (18in); the Hickman Chalice, 1608, height 33cm (13in).*

fits around the lemon container; the upper cup has a domed cover which projects beyond the rim of the cup and is hollowed out to hold spices. Still higher on the cover is a small cup which acts as a handle to it, and whose topmost portion is hollow to hold a nutmeg. Since all these parts screw together to form an ordered whole, it is an especially fine example of the turner's art.

Matching this last specimen is the
1 magnificent James VI and I standing cup, called the Hickman Chalice after a previous owner. Early 17th-century treen standing cups are much rarer than silver examples, and less than twenty are known to exist today. This one is made of fruitwood and has been elaborately turned on a lathe. Early pieces of treen were worked with adzes and chisels, but with the invention of the lathe more complicated shapes became possible. The turner would often hand his work over to another craftsman to complete the decoration. Here, a deep band of continuous leaf ornament, cross-hatched and deeply stylized, has been added around the body of the bowl. This has been raised and branded, probably with a hot needle.

Glass

The practical and decorative qualities of glass
have been exploited for over 3,000 years.
Glass is made by the fusion in a furnace of
silica, in the form of sand, flint or quartz, with
an alkaline flux which may be potash or soda.
These are the essential ingredients, but
limestone, chalk or oxides of lead may be
added to make the glass tougher and more
durable.

Throughout the Middle Ages, common
glass was made in many places in Germany
and the Rhineland. To be near a supply of
fuel, many of the glass furnaces were set up in
forests so the traditional type of glass made
there has come to be known as *Waldglas*,
meaning "forest glass". It could be either
green, yellow or brown in colour, and the
chief products of its early period were
domestic vessels, flasks and lamps, and phials
for apothecaries and alchemists.

Far into the 17th century, long after the
influence of Venetian glassmakers had swept
across Europe, the glass made in this region
remained virtually unchanged in appearance.
One of the most important types of *Waldglas*
was a cup or beaker with dropped-on spots of
1 glass on its stem. This glass, known as a
Römer, was the typical vessel for Rhenish
white wine. The example shown here, which
dates from the middle of the 17th century, has
a spreading foot formed by closely winding a
glass thread around a core which was later
removed. The bowl is engraved with the arms
of the seven provinces of the Netherlands
which united to form a republic in the 16th
century.

Other distinctive forms of glass, which
appeared at the same time as the *Römer* and
also persisted for several centuries, include
the tall, large beaker known as a *Humpen* and
its close relative, the *Passglas*, which was used
for communal drinking and was marked with
bands to indicate the amount to be drunk as
the glass was passed around the table. Due to
its size, the *Humpen* was a favourite object for
enamel decoration since it allowed plenty of
2 space to paint on. This example, dated 1693, is
broadly and robustly painted in bright,
opaque colours. Venetian decoration did

1 Römer, *Rhenish, c.1650, height 13.8cm (5½in).*

2 Humpen, *German, 1693, height 30.9cm (12⅛in).*

inspire German enamelling, which grew in popularity after the middle of the 16th century, by which time enamelling had gone out of fashion in Venice itself.

The Netherlands became the meeting place for many existing styles. Early Dutch glass owed much to Venetian styles and was in turn influenced by German and English trends and techniques. By the 18th century, English glass was copied and imported to such an extent that the Dutch glassmaking industry declined rapidly. Instead, the Dutch concentrated on the engraving of glass, a craft in which they excelled. The early examples of this work were largely executed by diamond-point engraving, a method that was succeeded by wheel engraving in the 18th century, and **3** a particularly fine flute decorated in this manner was purchased for the Collection in 1991. Showing an equestrian portrait of Prince William, who was later to become King of Great Britain, this flute was one of eighteen decorated Dutch glasses bought in that year. The craftsmen of Venice influenced glassmaking in Europe up to the 17th century. As their fame spread, skilled workers from this city were encouraged to settle in Germany, France, Spain and the Low Countries as well as England where it was not until the late 17th century that a recognisably English style could be distinguished. What provoked this development was the perfection of a new technique of glass manufacture. In 1763, in response to intensive efforts by the Glass Sellers' Company of London to free English glassworkers from the dependence on foreign raw materials, George Ravenscroft began experiments with materials obtainable in England. Silica, the basis of glass, was available from crushed flints but was difficult to fuse. Ravenscroft solved this problem by introducing a mixture of potash alkali and a lead oxide. When molten, this new glass, or metal, was physically heavier and less fluid than Venetian glass so could not be blown so thinly. It did, however, have the advantage of a brilliant light-refracting ability which is the special property of English glass and which resulted in a lead crystal of such quality that English glass reigned supreme for the next hundred years.

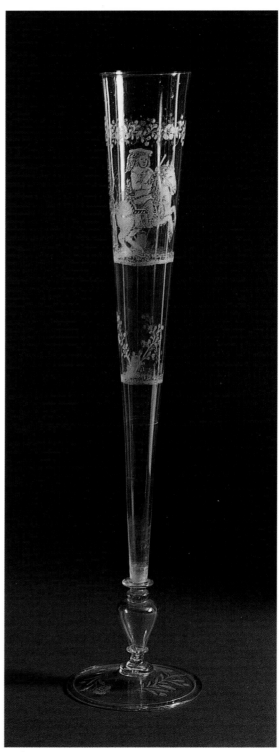

3 *Flute, Dutch, c.1660-5, height 50cm (18in).*

It is virtually impossible to date a glass other than by its shape and method of manufacture, but the Collection is rich in glasses whose stems reflect the varying trends and fashions of their periods. In the early years of the 18th century, wine glasses developed a large **4** variety of baluster stems. These examples date from between 1710 and 1720 and show globular, cylindrical, rectangular and true baluster knops.

4 *Wine glasses, English, c.1710-1720, heights 15.6cm (6⅛in), 14.6cm (5¾in) and 18.1cm (7⅛in).*

The trend towards lighter glasses and a corresponding emphasis on decoration were prompted by the Glass Excise Act of 1745 which imposed a levy on the weight of materials used, the money raised helping to pay for the wars against France. Bowls became smaller and stems more interesting visually. The process of manufacture was fairly simple: the bowl of glass was blown and the stem drawn out from it and worked into shape while the foot was attached separately. Around 1740, bubbles of air were introduced into the base of the bowl which was then drawn and spun simultaneously to draw out the air-twist stem. The addition of coloured **5** glass then led to the opaque-twist stem which followed around 1750. Apart from being physically lighter, designs too were more delicate, in keeping with the general taste of the time. Engraved glasses were used by various political factions throughout the 18th century, most notably by the Jacobites, and to commemorate important **6** national events. This rare goblet, which was probably made especially for the engraving, records the Battle of Trafalgar and its date of 21 October 1805.

5 *Wine glasses with air-twist (left and right) and opaque-twist (centre) stems, English, c.1740-1760, heights 17.2cm (6¾in), 15.6cm (6⅛in) and 20cm (7⅞in).*

6 *Commemorative goblet, English, 1805, height 21.3cm (8⅜in).*

Needlework

Needlework in England has a long and distinguished history going back to the early Middle Ages. Production before the Reformation was mainly for Church use, but afterwards it became more domestic.

Costume was a natural area for decorative needlework. The golden age of embroidered clothes in England was the Elizabethan era through to the middle of the 17th century when less elaborately embroidered garments were preferred. Fine embroidery was used mainly on jackets and smocks. This woman's jacket illustrates the heights it had reached by the years 1600 to 1625. Embroidered with coloured silks and plaited gold braid on a fine, cream-linen ground, it would have been worked professionally rather than by the lady of the house. Embroidered jackets, or bodices, remained in fashion for a long time and are the most complete articles of embroidered clothing to have survived. Accessories such as lace collars and cuffs were worn specifically to enhance the general effect of the jacket by complementing or contrasting with the flowery attractive scrolls of the embroidery.

From the list of New Year gifts received by Queen Elizabeth, we know that embroidered items were frequently used as presents. There is strong evidence to suggest, for example, that items of early 17th-century hawking equipment were given by King James VI and I to Sir William Pope after the King had visited Wroxton Abbey in Oxfordshire to act as godfather to one of Pope's children. They include a pouch, hoods, a gauntlet and lure, worked in gold, silver and coloured silks on leather. The clasp of the pouch is made of gold decorated with translucent enamels. The lure and the hoods may have come from a different set.

1 *Embroidered jacket, English, c.1600-1625, 48.2×45.7cm (19×18in).*

2 *Hawking pouch and gauntlet, English, early 17th century, length of gauntlet 38.1cm (15in).*

The quality of the hawking pieces suggests that they were also worked professionally. A large amount of work was, however, carried out by women who were expected to be proficient in needlework from an early age, and who were trained in stitches and skills by their mothers. Initially, girls worked samplers to record and practise various types of stitches, borders and motifs. As the name suggests, samplers were originally examples of different types of work and not the quaint pictures they were sometimes to become in Victorian times. The earliest surviving samplers date from the late 16th century. This example of c.1625-50 has been worked with coloured silks and silver thread on linen and incorporates five types of stitch: tent, rococo, Florentine, back-faggot filling and plaited-braid. By the mid-17th century, printed pattern books and engravings were being used to record various types of stitch, and the purpose of the sampler changed as the emphasis was placed more on its decorative role than its educational one.

Girls progressed from samplers to more ambitious work, such as embroidered pictures or small caskets covered by needlework. Pictures were very popular, and in the 17th century were sometimes padded to form stumpwork. The designs have a charming childish naivety about them, and frequently take their subject from the Bible. This box contains its original mirror inside and a number of drawers, probably for writing utensils, all lined in salmon-pink velvet and edged with silver braid. It dates from the latter half of the 17th century and illustrates an episode from the Book of Genesis, with Abraham's steward seeking a wife for Isaac. The Biblical characters appear somewhat incongruously in 17th-century costume and resemble Charles I and Henrietta Maria who, even after their deaths, were often used as models in allegorical scenes.

3 *Sampler with royal badges, English, c.1625-50, 52×33.5cm (20½×13¼in).*

4 *Embroidered casket, English, c.1650-1700, height 28.8cm (11⅜in).*

Furniture

An outstanding section of Sir William Burrell's Collection is the early furniture, of which there are some 500 pieces. During Burrell's lifetime, a large number were in use in the various rooms of Hutton Castle. Those in the Dining Room, Drawing Room and Hall are displayed in the reconstructions of these rooms and some of the more interesting are described in that chapter. In addition, other chests, cabinets and cupboards are shown in the Gothic, Domestic, Elizabethan and 17th-century period rooms.

Some articles can be directly associated with notable families as they come from their places of residence. In this historic context a particularly fine example is the Kimberley Throne, a composite piece from Kimberley Hall in Norfolk, which was the home of the Wodehouse family. By tradition the throne is associated with a visit made to Kimberley in 1578 by Queen Elizabeth I. The workmanship of different parts of the throne can be identified: the canopy, pelmets and frontal are the work of Italian or French craftworkers; by contrast, the underside of the canopy, which bears the arms of Sir Roger Wodehouse (d.1588) and his wife Mary Corbet, are of English make. These parts did not originally belong to the throne and are perhaps bed hangings. The throne is mentioned in the 1588 Inventory of Kimberley as having "crimson vellat with ye armes of Sir Roger Wodehouse

and [six] curteyns of clothe of sarcenet and vallence of red velvet fringed with red silk" The value given in the Inventory was 40 shillings.

A little earlier than the Kimberley Throne is a joined, long dining table in oak, of English make, which has elaborate inlays on the top. The arms of the Brome and Crossley families appear in escutcheons in the corners, while

2 *Walnut bureau cabinet, English, c.1705, height 228.2cm (89⅞in), width 99cm (39in), depth 59.7cm (23½in).*

1 *Detail of the Kimberley Throne, English, Italian or French, 16th century.*

3 *Fireplace and overmantel, English, mid-16th century, height 305cm (120¼in).*

the date, 1569, and the cyphers IB and MB feature in the centre. This table, apart from having six legs instead of four and differences in the inlaid designs, is very similar to the so-called Nonsuch table belonging to the Duke of Devonshire, to be seen at Hardwick Hall in Derbyshire.

Occupying a prominent position on the north wall of the same room are a splendid oak

3 fireplace and overmantel which reputedly came from the Tudor royal palace of Oatlands, near Weybridge in Surrey, and were acquired in 1953 from the Hearst Collection. The central panel features the royal arms of the Tudors. The elaborate carvings include lions, dragons, caryatids, human figures, mermaids and serpents, arranged in a decorative design. The rose and lily, the floral emblems of England

and France, are a reminder of the English monarchy's claim to reign over both countries.

Belonging to the early 18th century and exhibited in the room containing the 17th and 18th-century paintings, is a magnificent

2 bureau cabinet, a very fine specimen of the cabinetmaker's art from the Queen Anne period. Made of walnut, about 1705, it formerly belonged to the Countess of Carlisle, of Castle Howard in Yorkshire. On top, the cornice supports five carved and gilded figures. Below, double doors open to reveal vertical compartments, a central cupboard and drawers, while the lower part has a fall front and various drawers. The surfaces throughout are veneered with figured burr walnut.

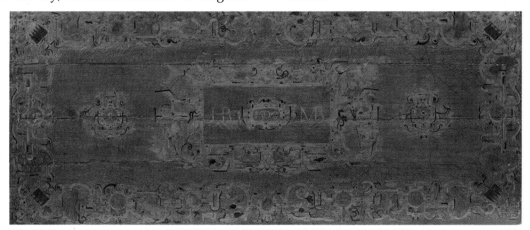

4 *Oak table, English, 1569, height 90.2cm (35½in), length 223.6cm (88in), width 102.9cm (40½in).*

There are more chairs in the Collection than any other type of furniture. These range from sets of dining chairs to single luxurious or unusual examples. Among upholstered 5 chairs an English winged armchair dating from about 1700 stands out. The frame is walnut, but it is the hand-embroidered fabric used to cover the chair that is really special. The embroidered scenes on the back of the chair depict the Apocryphal stories of Suannah and the Elders (above) and Hagar fed by the ravens (below).

6 Such scenes were commonly embroidered on small panels used as pictures or cushion covers, but rarely employed on such a large scale. It was much commoner to find upholstery fabric with an all-over design.

At the other extreme of comfort (though they would have been used with cushions) are various rustic or regional wooden

6 *Detail of embroidery on the back.*

chairs, most of them decorated with carved 7 or turned features. An outstanding and rare turned chair dated 1685 is of ash and was probably made in the south west of England. Carved panels bear the name of George Shillibeare (of whom nothing further is known) which makes this an unusual example of a documentary chair incorporating both turned and carved decoration.

5 *Embroidered chair, English, c.1700, height 122.5cm, width 81.3cm, depth 58.4cm (48¼in × 32in × 23in).*

7 *Turned oak chair, English, 1685, height 119.4cm, width 59.7cm, depth 44.5cm (47in × 23½in × 17½in).*

Paintings

Paintings were among the first objects that Sir William Burrell acquired for his Collection, and he was still buying them two years before his death. The Collection is deservedly renowned for its holding of 19th-century French painting, including some magnificent Impressionist gems. The strength of this area has tended to overshadow other smaller sections, such as the group of Northern Renaissance paintings which includes important Memlings and Cranachs, while the small number of Dutch 17th-century works is crowned by Rembrandt's *Self-Portrait.* The Collection would have been wider still had Sir William not sold some paintings early in this century, including two major works by Whistler, *The Fur Jacket* and *La Princesse du Pays de la Porcelaine,* which now adorn museums in the United States.

Burrell's collecting pattern before 1911, the date of the first purchase books, remains somewhat obscure. It is certain that he had already amassed a large collection, judging from his loans to the 1901 Glasgow International Exhibition. It is also evident that the Hague School dominated his taste at that time. The explanation for this can be found in the presence of the dealer Craibe Angus in Glasgow from 1874. Through his family association with Matthijs Maris and the Dutch dealer van Wisselingh, Craibe Angus introduced the Hague and Barbizon Schools to Scottish buyers.

Burrell was a man of firm likes and dislikes, but he was prepared to take advice from dealers he trusted. The most important figure in this respect was Alexander Reid, who opened a gallery in Glasgow in 1889 and from whom Burrell bought consistently until the 1920s. Reid had spent a number of years in Paris, and had even shared lodgings with Vincent Van Gogh. He brought to Glasgow a large stock of canvases by Corot, Courbet, Daumier, Boudin and Degas as well as the more profitable contemporary Dutch works.

Sir William was a cautious man, and it can be assumed that initially he had a preference for low-toned pictures and a corresponding distrust of the bolder flights of Impressionist painting. While he did buy a Degas around 1901, he offered it for sale in 1902 and twenty of the twenty-two works by Degas in the Collection were bought in the 1920s and 1930s, after the artist's death. Burrell's first purchases of French art were works by Daumier, Bargue, Monticelli, Ribot and Bonvin, which are all indications of his conservative taste.

It was between 1915 and 1926 that Burrell began to acquire the majority of his French pictures, when they were amongst the most expensive items he was buying. A vintage year was 1926 when he purchased Daumier's *The Miller, his Son and the Ass,* Degas' *The Rehearsal* and Manet's *Women Drinking Beer.* Thereafter, Burrell did not acquire paintings so intensively, but was always ready to buy should anything exceptional come on to the market. In 1937 he bought two more masterpieces, Cézanne's *Château de Médan* and Degas' *Jockeys in the Rain.* These pictures were among the last he bought from the gallery of Reid and Lefevre. As far as French painting was concerned, his picture buying was at an end, but he continued to add outstanding pictures to other areas. In 1946 Rembrandt's *Self-Portrait* entered the Collection at a cost of £12,500. This figure was exceeded two years later when he bought Frans Hals's *Portrait of a Gentleman* for £14,500, the highest sum he ever spent on any one item.

One artist Burrell never tired of was Joseph Crawhall. Crawhall was born in the same year as Burrell and shared the same Northumbrian roots as the Burrell family, which perhaps explains Burrell's constant acquisition of Crawhall's watercolours from his very earliest buying days.

Detail from The Prancing Grey Horse *by Théodore Géricault.*

Early Paintings

The 15th century saw a reorientation in European art. About the middle of that century, artists began to examine the outward appearance of things with fresh eyes. The beauties of landscape, the human face and everyday subjects were lovingly and painstakingly depicted. The artists of Northern Europe, and particularly the Low Countries, played a leading role in this movement towards the literal depiction of reality, aided by an important technical advance. It was Flemish painters who first followed the lead of Jan van Eyck and used oil to bind their colours together rather than water or white of egg. The resulting paint was slower drying so artists could be more deliberate in their execution, and it produced deeper, more brilliant colours which added a liveliness missing from earlier methods.

This major development brought with it a new approach to which artists had to adapt the old traditions of religious pictures.

1 In *The Adoration of the Magi* the Master of the Prado Adoration of the Magi shows an ordinary domestic interior of around 1460, which would have seemed homely and familiar to the painter's fellow citizens of Bruges. By placing the Virgin Mary in this room the artist has created a world where imagination and reality are fused. Originally, this panel formed the right wing of a triptych altarpiece whose other panels are to be found in Madrid and Washington.

Rapid changes came over the art of Northern Europe as ideas from the Italian Renaissance were absorbed. Artists looked for a wider range of subjects than those offered by religion, whose role was also undergoing changes. The teachings of Martin Luther had prompted several countries to break away from the authority of the pope, and the resulting greater intellectual freedom made itself felt in painting as in the other arts.

Landscapes became increasingly common, and outdoor events were placed in settings which had recognizable dimensions but

2 nevertheless were idealized, as in *The Stag Hunt* by Lucas Cranach the Elder (1472-1533). An artist of religious pictures, portraits, and

1 *The Master of the Prado Adoration of the Magi*
The Adoration of the Magi, *panel 58.5×35cm (23×14in).*

woodcuts, in 1504 Cranach was called to the court of Saxony where he remained as a court painter to the end of his life. He was highly successful and had no shortage of commissions since he was a close friend of Martin Luther and the artist *par excellence* of the Reformation. It was in his capacity as official artist that he painted this hunt scene for the Elector John the Constant, who is seen in the bottom right corner. The other huntsmen in the foreground with their courtiers have been identified as Frederick the Wise of Saxony and the Holy Roman Emperor Maximilian I, both of whom had died by 1529 when the picture was painted. This, then, is a memorial picture of a real event, with all the figures individual people, not faceless actors. Another fine work by Cranach is *Judith with the Head of Holofernes*, painted in 1530. The Apochryphal Jewish heroine is shown, dressed in scarlet finery, posed dramatically against a landscape background and holding the bloodied sword with which she beheaded the enemy commander who posed a threat to her people.

2 *Lucas Cranach the Elder* The Stag Hunt, *1529, panel 83.2×119.5cm (32¾×47in).*

Sir William Burrell preferred the Late Gothic art and artefacts of Northern Europe to those of Renaissance Italy, but among his small group of Italian paintings special **3** mention must be made of the *Virgin and Child* by Giovanni Bellini (*c.* 1430-1516) which had rested in the Palazzo Barberini in Rome for over four hundred years before Burrell acquired it in 1930. The art of the Renaissance heralded a new approach to the world, with mankind the measure of all things. Artists began to assert their own personalities through their painting and formulated new visual principles based on precise mathematical and geometrical laws. Simultaneously, purely aesthetic aspects of art came to be recognized and enjoyed for their own sake. For example, here Bellini takes an essentially simple composition and gives it life through a sense of motion, created by suspending a flower from a thread. By using this device to make both figures seem unaware of their great spiritual significance, the painter has created a more human and forceful image than those within the scope of pre-Renaissance religious painters.

3 *Giovanni Bellini* Virgin and Child, *c.1488-90, panel 62.2×47.6cm (24½×18¾in).*

Dutch and British Paintings

Aside from his passion for French painting, Sir William Burrell cultivated a taste for Dutch art from both the 17th and 19th centuries. The concern for detail which had pervaded early Netherlandish painting provided the roots for the flowering of Dutch painting in the 17th century. There were important changes, however. Although the great majority of early Netherlandish painting had had a religious content, several factors combined to alter the subject matter in later Dutch art. The Reformation had taken its effect, and the Protestant view of religious art was defined by Calvin who declared: "Man should not paint or carve anything except what he sees around him, so that God's majesty may not be corrupted by fantasies." Nor did cultural life centre on the royal court as it did in England and France. Instead, the growth through trade, shipping and industry of a prosperous middle class had created new wealth and made it possible for many people to decorate their homes with pictures. They chose scenes which depicted their surroundings as well as still lifes and portraits. Art flourished through the contentment and vitality of the well-to-do burgher, such as the one painted by Frans

2 Hals (1581/5-1666) in his *Portrait of a Gentleman* of around 1639. Hals used a full brush loaded with paint which he applied in broad, rapid strokes that kept the freshness of a sketch and prevented his sitters from becoming bored or tired. Thus his portraits seem very natural, as if he has caught not only the facial likeness of his models but also their characteristic stances and attitudes.

Many artists specialized in just one area, which is why the standard of work throughout this period is so high. There were landscape painters, seascape painters, animal painters; others did interiors or just church interiors; and some concentrated on still lifes consisting only of flowers. But one artist excelled in almost all these fields: Rembrandt van Rijn (1606-69). The son of a miller, Rembrandt was born in Leiden and set up there as a local painter in the late 1620s. In order to fulfil his ambitions as a society portrait painter, he moved to Amsterdam in

1 1631. The *Self-Portrait* was painted in the following year and shows a smart, fashionably dressed young man, no doubt a good advertisement for prospective clients. The polished and tightly executed style also marks a change from his previous work which had been of a looser and more vigorous manner unlikely to appeal to the sophisticated tastes of Amsterdam. The portrait was once in the French royal collection before it was sold in London in 1792 by the notorious Duke of Orléans, together with other Dutch and Flemish pictures. The Duke, better known as Philippe Egalité, was a debauched member of the Bourbon family, who voted for the death of Louis XVI. He was guillotined in 1793 after suspicions that he desired the throne.

Rembrandt is rightly renowned for the psychological depth of his portraits as well as for their technical brilliance. He used himself as a model throughout his life, leaving a

1 *Rembrandt van Rijn* Self-Portrait, *1632, panel 63.5 ×46.3cm (24¾×18½in).*

2 *Frans Hals* Portrait of a Gentleman, *c.1639, canvas 117×91.5cm (46×36in).*

unique record of his facial, mental and stylistic progress. The early self-portraits often show him grimacing or laughing, as if they were exercises in depicting various emotions. Others, like the Burrell portrait, reveal his professional progress while later portraits are

3 *William Hogarth* Mrs Ann Lloyd, *c.1744, canvas 76.2×63.5cm (30×25in)*.

4 *Sir Henry Raeburn* Miss Macartney, *c.1794, canvas 73.7×61cm (29×24in)*.

private and powerful revelations of his personality. The Collection also possesses four Rembrandt prints, one of which is illustrated on page 154.

Housed with the Dutch 17th-century paintings is a selection of British portraits from the 18th century. Between 1500 and 1700 the best artists working in Britain were foreign. Patrons controlled the market and seemed only to want idealized likenesses of themselves wearing fine jewels and clothes, reflecting their position in life. Flemish, Dutch and German names predominate, from Holbein to Kneller. It was the ambition of William Hogarth (1696-1764) to create an independent, recognizably English school of painting, which would rival and hopefully surpass all other schools, and it is for this reason that he is traditionally referred to as the father of British painting. He attempted to achieve this superiority by producing history paintings and a series of canvases illustrating both the vices and virtues of contemporary life. In his opinion, portrait painting was a pretty contemptible affair since it dealt with flattery and did not touch upon any of the higher things in life. Despite this, Hogarth produced some excellent portraits which are 3 far from being dull and one of which is in the Collection.

The painting of portraits remained, theoretically, a second-class occupation for artists in England throughout the century, an attitude which was reinforced by Sir Joshua Reynolds. As President of the Royal Academy, Reynolds gave annual lectures to the students, which were published as *The Discourses* and summarize 18th-century artistic thought. In these lectures he maintained that art was superior to nature and should lift the spectator's mind above the mere physical world. This meant that landscapes and people became idealized pastiches of themselves, and artists used the recognized old masters as sources for their work. This led to a considerable aridity in academic art which tended to consist of large-scale history pictures that were totally unsaleable. Portrait painting, however, flourished with the increasing wealth created by the industrial revolution and trade abroad. Sitters were not too concerned with the niceties of high art, just wanting competent 4 likenesses of themselves. *Miss Macartney* by Sir Henry Raeburn (1756-1823) is a typical late 18th-century portrait. Raeburn lived and worked in Edinburgh and so avoided the fierce competition among the London artists like Lawrence, Hoppner, Beechey and Opie. He was largely self-taught, and the broad, sweeping treatment he evolved was designed to create a general effect. If his paintings sometimes lack detail, they are always solid and convincing images.

The Hague School

Sir William Burrell's early taste in painting was fairly conventional and lay with the contemporary masters of the Hague School. By 1870, the Hague had become an enthusiastic centre for a group of young painters described by that name. These artists never experienced the rejection or fight for recognition that bedevilled the French Impressionists, although they shared the same artistic intentions and goals. This similarity was brought about by dealers in the Hague, like H. J. van Wisselingh and his son, and the Hague subsidiary of the Parisian firm of Goupil, who introduced and popularized French art. Painters like Courbet, Corot and members of the Barbizon School, who were the precursors of Impressionism, were well known and admired in Holland, and in emulation of these painters the Dutch artists used landscape as the vehicle for their art.

Like their more famous counterparts, they were preoccupied with the portrayal of light and the sensations to be derived from colour, form and movement. There was, however, a strong streak of conservatism in their work, which proved acceptable to bourgeois taste. The difference between the Hague School artists and others, from Amsterdam for example, is explained by the training these artists received. In the Hague there was close contact between older and younger artists, because the latter completed their apprenticeships in the studio of an experienced painter. The result was that new ideas were slowly assimilated. The Hague School artists did not face a struggle with an autocratic academy, nor was their behaviour in any sense radical and so did not dissuade potential patrons. The consequence was that they came to be regarded as the leading artistic innovators of their day.

1 The caution of the Hague School is evident in the limited range of colours used in *Carting Sand* by Anton Mauve (1838-1888). His pictures consist of unpretentious subjects from country life, and he repeatedly used the same light, silvery colours. Unlike that of the Realists of France, his work makes no comment on the working conditions of the

1 *Anton Mauve* Carting Sand, *c.1880, canvas 35.5×53.5cm (14×21in).*

peasantry, nor are they about the integrity of hard work. They are merely excercises in the graduation of colour and tone. Nowadays, Mauve is perhaps better remembered as the cousin of Vincent Van Gogh, who spent some time in his studio in 1883. Although Van Gogh was impressed by the sincerity of Mauve as an artist, he did not remain long there as he found the colours used by the Hague artists totally unsatisfactory for his own work.

The leading characters of the Hague School were the Maris brothers, Jacob (1837-99), Matthijs (1839-1917) and Willem (1848-1910), all of whom are well represented in the Collection. Jacob excelled at town and harbour
2 scenes, and his *Amsterdam* exists in several versions. Like Mauve, he used a restricted palette with a dominant note of pearl grey or golden brown to create his effects. Jacob's earliest work had been figural subjects in the style of Dutch 17th-century painting, then in 1865 he travelled to Paris and remained there for six years, coming under the direct influence of Corot and Jongkind. Amongst the Hague School group, Jacob Maris' work most closely resembles the paintings of the Impressionists. Unlike them, however, Jacob executed his canvases from beginning to end in his studio, thus they are more finished and invariably larger than Impressionist pictures. In order to catch the immediacy of their sensations, the Impressionists had to paint at great speed and out of doors. This meant small-scale pictures with the look of sketches.

2 *Jacob Maris* Amsterdam, *c.1885, canvas 81.3×146cm (32×57½in).*

Unlike the Dutch painters, they were not prepared to elaborate or to enlarge their initial ideas. This remains the essential difference between the two schools.

Matthijs Maris' work stands distinctly apart from his brothers' and the rest of the Hague School because his paintings took on a visionary and dreamlike quality. He received the same artistic training as his brother Jacob and followed him to Paris in 1867 before settling permanently in London in 1872. His early work contains the Impressionist elements common to the group, but he rapidly developed an ethereal side to both his nature and his painting. In *The Sisters* of 1875 the beginning of this transition can be seen. His figures remain solid and are not the shadowy spectres they were to become, yet the background remains ill-defined and no attempt is made to describe the landscape. The whole work has a wistfulness which proved popular to late 19th-century taste.

3

Sir William Burrell acquired over fifty paintings, drawings and prints by Matthijs Maris. This surprisingly large quantity was due to his popularity in Scotland and particularly Glasgow. Maris was a very private man and one of his few friends was the British dealer Craibe Angus. In 1887, E. J. van Wisselingh married Craibe Angus' daughter, who cared for the painter until his death in 1917. As early as 1874, Craibe Angus had set up a gallery in Glasgow and had introduced

3 *Matthijs Maris* The Sisters, *1875, canvas 99.1×62.2cm (39×24½in).*

Matthijs Maris and other artists of the Hague School to Scotland. Burrell would have been familiar with their work, and these paintings were among his first purchases. The influx of work by the Hague School had a substantial influence on Scottish painting and in particular in the early years of this century on the Glasgow Boys.

French Paintings

The earliest independent French school of painting began with those artists born between 1580 and 1600, such as Poussin, Claude Lorrain, Blanchard and Vouet. The artistic unity France experienced at the beginning of the 17th century was part of a wider sense of order and unity throughout the country as a whole. In 1635, Cardinal Richelieu founded the Académie Française, which was intended to act as a focal point for the arts and sciences. The Académie Royale de Peinture et de la Sculpture, or the Academy, followed in 1648, and it was around or against this body that painting developed in France in the succeeding centuries. In official circles of the time, the fashion was for large-scale mythological and religious paintings, but some artists were evolving a more personal

2 *Jean-Baptiste Chardin* Still Life, *c.1729, canvas 27.9×36.8cm (11×14½in).*

render the texture of objects and his matter-of-fact realism made him a lasting favourite and a highly influential figure in
2 later French painting. His still lifes are in stark contrast to the prevailing rococo taste with its hints of decadence.

Many naturalistic works, however, had a
3 purely decorative role. The striking picture of a dog by Jean-Baptiste Oudry (1696-1755) was intended to be set in a fireplace during the summer months to exclude the draught and to give the impression of a real dog standing

1 *Antoine le Nain* Peasant Children, *c.1630-1640, copper 21.6×27.9cm (8½×11in).*

view of the world, including Antoine le Nain
1 (1588-1648), the artist of *Peasant Children*.

By the end of the 17th century, academic art was sharply divided between the followers of Poussin, who favoured intellectual painting and the importance of line over colour, and the supporters of Rubens, who preferred colour and more sensual works. Burrell did not collect examples of either of these schools but favoured more naturalistic painters like Jean-Baptiste Chardin (1699-1779) who took their inspiration from the commonplace things in everyday life. Chardin's ability to

3 *Jean-Baptiste Oudry* The Dog, *1751, canvas 90.2×113.1cm (35½×44½in).*

there. Such was Oudry's skill in portraying animals that he was appointed to the esoteric position of animal painter and painter of the royal hunts to Louis XV, in addition to being the director of the Beauvais tapestry factory.

The late 18th century saw the challenging of many of the established political, social and philosophical orders of Europe, particularly in France where it culminated in the French Revolution. The arts of that century, which had catered largely for the ruling elite, were considered amoral and frivolous, and it was felt that a new disciplined style would get them back on to rational lines. The Revolution provided the ideal climate for such a change, and Neoclassicism came to be adopted in official artistic circles. In painting this style was based on hard outlines and minute finishing, derived from a re-examination of the classical art of ancient Greece and Rome. Neoclassicism also came to stand for wider moral issues, so that to paint in an abandoned manner carried with it connotations of immorality. Painters became involved in politics, and clashes between artists and with authority were commonplace throughout the 19th century, with repercussions for men like Courbet, Daumier and the Impressionists.

At the beginning of the century, however, some artists were already against this intellectual and excessively rational attitude to art and championed a freer approach which put more emphasis on the imagination and the senses. This movement came to be known
4 as Romanticism, and *The Prancing Grey Horse* by Théodore Géricault (1791-1824), painted in 1812, embodies its lively and fiery spirit – even the paint, thickly and quickly applied, seems in sympathy with the theme. Géricault's art was entirely free of learned principles and dogmatic ideas. It was formed instead by the impressions of his early youth in his native town of Rouen, and particularly his fondness for horses. Because of his early death, Géricault's art never reached full maturity. Instead, the ideas of Romanticism were realized by a slightly younger man, Eugène Delacroix (1798–1863), who was a fellow pupil of Géricault in 1816 in the studio of Guérin, and who openly expressed his admiration for the older painter. Géricault's masterpiece, *The Raft of the Medusa,* now in the Louvre in Paris, made a deep impression on Delacroix who

4 *Théodore Géricault* The Prancing Grey Horse, *1812, canvas 45.1×54.6cm (17¾×21½in).*

5 *Eugène Delacroix* The White Horse, *c.1823, canvas 45.7×55.9cm (18×22in).*

recounted how he ran home "mad" with enthusiasm when he saw it half-completed in
5 Géricault's studio. *The White Horse* of *c.*1823 was painted in emulation of Géricault, and it is said that Delacroix particularly treasured this early work. Delacroix's later work represents a complete break from traditional techniques in that he used colour not as the accidental property of an object but for its own expressive qualities.

Despite the advances made by the Romantic artists, the Academy, under the direction of Ingres, continued to favour Neoclassical tastes, which meant a predilection for large-scale historical or mythological scenes with meticulous finishes. The artists who did challenge the assumptions of the Academy

6 *Gustave Courbet* The Charity of a Beggar at Ornans, *1868, canvas 210.9×175.3cm (83×69in).*

did so especially forcefully, since up to the 1880s that body maintained a grip on the official Salon whose annual exhibition remained the only practical way an artist could reach a wide public. Gradually more artists began to question the subjects that were being painted and to think about new methods of applying paint to canvas. Stuffy pictures of dim events were considered outmoded, and real, everyday scenes were **6** judged to be more relevant to art. *The Charity of a Beggar at Ornans* by Gustave Courbet (1819-77) is an example of this new challenge. Such unconventional paintings of peasant life had political overtones, and Courbet's radicalism eventually led him to a term of imprisonment. He frequently came under attack both for the crude technique of his pictures and for their content, although he did achieve a fair amount of public success.

Painters of contemporary life were not all confined to Courbet's brand of social realism. Honoré Daumier (1808-79) treated similar subjects with a sympathy and an understanding of the harshness of life, as in **7** *The Heavy Burden*. During his lifetime Daumier was better known for the political and social caricatures he published in various periodicals rather than for his canvases. Although he was accepted four times at the Salon, his paintings never achieved critical success and remained practically unknown until an exhibition a year before his death, when he was nearly blind and penniless. The Collection possesses several oil paintings by Daumier and also nine

8 *Jean François Millet* The Shepherdess, *1849, panel 29.8×16.5cm (11¾×6½in).*

Jean François Millet's pictures have a quiet, reflective quality and make no grand statements about life. Millet (1814-75) produced the bulk of his work in the village of Barbizon, near the Forest of Fontainebleau, away from the stresses and problems of **8** Parisian life. Millet's view of rural life conveys an almost Biblical quality by his emphasis on the nobility and honesty of working with the soil. While he too suffered rejection at official hands, he eventually won a first-class medal at the Salon and was awarded the Légion d'Honneur. The landscape around Barbizon attracted many artists who developed a naturalistic style. This group took the name of the Barbizon School and included Daubigny, Jacque and Corot.

Side-by-side with these new themes, more

7 *Honoré Daumier* The Heavy Burden, *1855/6, canvas 39.3×31.3cm (15½×12¼in).*

watercolours and drawings, one of which is illustrated on page 155.

Other artists adopted yet another approach to the painting of contemporary life.

9 *François Bonvin* Still Life, *1884, canvas 32.4×42.5cm (12¾×16¾in).*

10 *Henri Fantin-Latour* Chrysanthemums, *1874, canvas 55.2×64.8cm (21¾×25½in).*

traditional subjects continued to be popular with artists. François Bonvin (1817-87)
9 specialized in still lifes and was credited by his contemporaries with the revival of this branch of art. He was largely self-taught and relied heavily on the example of Chardin in arranging his compositions. Unlike those of other members of the Realist group, Bonvin's subjects could hardly arouse antagonism. It was perhaps the docile nature of his work that made him acceptable, and he received a large number of commissions. This placed him in a prominent and important position among the Realists, a position he used to assist other, aspiring artists. In 1859, when a number of young painters were rejected by the Salon, Bonvin exhibited their works in his studio. One man he helped in this way was another highly talented still-life painter, Henri Fantin-Latour (1836-1904). The name of Fantin-Latour is traditionally associated with flower paintings, yet Fantin saw these works only as a means of livelihood. He believed

that the proper nature of painting lay with large-scale fantasies inspired by the music of Brahms, Wagner, Schumann and Berlioz, fantasies which had as little appeal then as now. His delightful flowerpieces were nearly all destined for the British market and remained virtually unknown in his native France until a retrospective exhibition in 1906,
10 after his death. *Chrysanthemums* once belonged to the painter Edwin Edwards who became unofficial business manager for Fantin and secured a steady income for him in England from his portraits and still lifes. Fantin-Latour did not share the ideas of his contemporaries on art. He fell out with Courbet, Legros and Whistler, and his admiration for Manet waned after that painter became involved with the Impressionists whom he also disliked. Aside from his awkward personality, the reason for his alienation from his fellow artists was his belief that art and contemporary life must never be united. This ran against the drift of general

11 *Eugène Boudin* The Empress Eugénie on the Beach at Trouville, *1863, wood 34.2×57.8cm (13½×22¾in).*

12 *Edouard Manet* Women Drinking Beer, *1878, pastel on linen 60.9×50.8cm (24×20in).*

opinion so he remained somewhat apart from the changes and innovations of the time.

The greatest artistic revolution of the 19th century was the result of developments in the handling of paint by those artists called the Impressionists. As a cohesive movement Impressionism is confined to the 1870s, yet its origins lay amid the wider naturalistic movement which had begun some thirty or forty years before. What so vigorously challenged the precepts of the Academy was the group's ideas on pictorial naturalism whereby subject matter was reduced to strictly visual factors. *The Empress Eugénie on the Beach at Trouville* of 1863 by Eugène Boudin (1824-98) illustrates this new uncomplicated vision which was the basis of Impressionist thinking. There are no grand gestures, complicated compositional features or hidden messages, merely the straightforward recording of what has been seen. Although the title tells us that the beautiful Spanish wife of the Emperor Napoleon III is present, it is hard to distinguish which figure she is since Boudin makes the real subject of his painting the morning light and the sea breeze. As demonstrated in this painting, Boudin laid many of the foundation stones of Impressionism by lightening the palette, allowing the sky to flood the picture, by creating greater freedom in composition, and by his strong interest in light and movement. Boudin's most typical and successful pictures show the harbours and beaches of northern France – Fécamp, Honfleur, Le Havre, Deauville and Trouville – with the shipping of the ports and the colourful crinolines of the fashionably dressed patrons of these resorts.

By common consent, Edouard Manet (1832-83) is regarded as the leader of the Impressionist group, but this description is not strictly accurate since he never properly shared their attitude to nature. Rather, he was the rallying point for the group, particularly after the Salon des Refusés in 1863. In that year, 3,000 artists submitted 5,000 paintings and sculptures to the official Salon, of which only 2,000 were accepted. After several appeals, the Emperor permitted another exhibition of the rejected paintings. In this exhibition Manet's pictures caused a furore, especially *Le Déjeuner sur l'herbe*, now in the Louvre in Paris, which caused such notoriety that he became the hero of the avant-garde. Today it is difficult to see what is so radical about his work, but in terms of technique the abrupt contrasts of tone opposed the smooth and gradual transitions of the academic tradition and were a revelation, together with his loose, even rough, handling of paint.

A sense of common purpose was generated by the discussions and arguments that took place in the Paris cafés of the time. These were important meeting places for artists, writers and intellectuals of all sorts. They also provided excellent material for many artists, and Manet drew on them extensively, in drawings, oil paintings and pastels, as in his **12** *Women Drinking Beer* of 1878. .

The progression towards a more natural and uncomplicated type of vision meant that any object or mundane scene could form the **13** basis of a picture. *Fabrique de Cuirs Forts*, painted in 1868 by Johan Barthold Jongkind (1819-91), shows the demolition of a factory in one of Paris's industrial suburbs and is almost deliberately anti-picturesque. A few years previously, in 1863, Baudelaire had published an essay called ''The Painter of Modern Life'' in which he maintained that it was precisely this sort of detached vision that best reflected the essential characteristics of the age. Jongkind was a Dutchman and, like van Gogh's, his art came to fruition in France rather than Holland through the stimulus of Impressionism. This canvas is one of several pictures showing the same view under different conditions of light, because the Impressionists had discovered that light controls colour, mood and even form.

The idea of painting light itself was central **14** to the painters of Impressionism. *The Bell Tower at Noisy-le-Roi: Autumn* by Alfred Sisley (1839-89) originally had the title *Autumn Morning* to emphasize the artist's interest in a particular season and a specific time of day. Sisley, who was of English parentage, exhibited at four Impressionist Exhibitions, including the first in 1874, the year this picture was painted. These exhibitions were a series of shows organized independently by the artists in an attempt to establish themselves after continued rejection and discouragement from the official Salon. The consequence was that within ten years no artist could ignore the advances being made by the Impressionists. One of the immediate effects of this influence was a transformation in the treatment of colour, from the dark and light values of the

13 *Johan Barthold Jongkind* Fabrique de Cuirs Forts, *1868 canvas 34.3×42.5cm (13½×16¾in).*

14 *Alfred Sisley* The Bell Tower at Noisy-le-Roi: Autumn, *1874, canvas 45.7×61cm (18×24in).*

Realists to brilliant hues and light tones. The Impressionists overturned the Academic principle of modelling with different tones of the same colour and instead brought into play a whole range of different colours, even in the shadows of a sunlit scene. In Sisley's picture, notice how he uses delicate blues in the shaded areas under the trees.

As Impressionist colour became richer and more varied, it began to have less contact with normal visual perceptions. Artists began to

15 *Paul Cézanne* Le Château de Médan, *c.1880, canvas 59×72.4cm (23¼×28½in).*

16 *Edgar Degas* The Rehearsal, *c.1877, canvas 58.4×83.8cm (23×33in).*

One of the clearest indications of Burrell's taste in art is given by his admiration for Degas who is represented by over twenty paintings, pastels and drawings. Edgar Degas (1834-1917) epitomized the intellectual approach to painting. "What I do," he told the Irish writer George Moore, "is the result of reflection and the study of the great masters; spontaneity, inspiration and temperament mean nothing to me." Degas left nothing to chance, and such seemingly casual **16** compositions as *The Rehearsal* were carefully and deliberately planned, and he was greatly influenced by Japanese coloured prints in his use of the unexpected angle and unusual cut-off points. Here, the centre of the canvas, where one would normally expect to find the subject of the painting, is empty and the action takes place at the sides and rear. The spiral staircase has been introduced because of its interesting shape and rigid geometry which provide a foil to the billowy dresses of the ballerinas on the right. It is by these balancing and contrasting interplays that Degas creates a sense of unity.

Degas had a detailed knowledge of the history of art, which he had studied on trips to Florence and Naples between 1854 and 1859. He had the highest regard for Ingres, the leading representative of Neoclassical painting, and his early works were in the historical genre. In 1862, he came under the influence of Manet and of the novelist and critic Edmond Duranty, a passionate believer in realism who in 1856 founded a magazine **17** called *Le Réalisme* and whose portrait by Degas is one of the masterpieces of Impressionism. The two men shared many ideas. Duranty believed that in portraiture the sitter should be shown in the clothes, surroundings and activities peculiar to him in everyday life. Consequently, Degas has portrayed the man of letters against a kaleidoscopic background of books; even the bottle of ink and the two magnifying glasses give us clues to the man's interests.

Degas contributed ten works to the first group show mounted by the Impressionists and exhibited at all the others except in 1882. In 1886, after the eighth and final group exhibition, Degas stopped sending his works to public shows altogether. His eyesight had deteriorated, and he worked more and more

think more and more about the process and method of making a picture rather than trying **15** to recreate nature. *Le Château de Médan*, by Paul Cézanne (1839-1906), was painted while the artist was staying with the writer and critic Emile Zola at his house at Médan, on the Seine, northwest of Paris. The brushwork forms an ordered pattern which underlies the two-dimensionality of the painting, for Cézanne believed the eye should combine with the intellect. The eye perceives nature and the intellect imposes a logical order on that sensation, and from the interplay of these two expression comes. Cézanne remained faithful to many aspects of Impressionism, but the complexity of his temperament manifested itself through his painting in an obsession with order and structure.

17 *Edgar Degas* Edmond Duranty, *1879, tempera, watercolour and pastel on linen 100×100cm (39¾×39½in).*

in pastel which he found easier to handle and with which he was able to render bold effects.

The worlds of ballet and horse racing supplied Degas with an inexhaustible quantity of material. He was not a particularly keen follower of these pursuits, rather it was the shapes that these subjects yielded and their movements which fascinated him.

18 Around 1886, Degas drew *Jockeys in the Rain* in which his constant preoccupation with the careful arrangement of space is once again evident. The blank triangle of grass on the left acts as a foil to a similar triangle of horses and riders on the right. Degas executed a number of drawings and pastels to arrive at this composition in which nothing is haphazard. Instead of a generalized vision, he presents movement frozen in time.

18 *Edgar Degas* Jockeys in the Rain, *c.1886, pastel 47×63.5cm (18½×25in).*

Prints and Drawings

There is a varied assortment of prints and drawings in the Collection which supplements the main body of pictures and among which is a small number of old-master
1 etchings and woodcuts. *The Death of the Virgin* of 1510 is a fine example of Albrecht Dürer's graphic art. It forms part of a series of woodcuts of the Life of the Virgin which Dürer (1471-1528) had begun over five years before. Over this period, his style had become simplified and geared to a general effect. Here, light moves across from the right and gives a general cohesiveness to the print which his earlier work had lacked. Dürer excelled in woodcutting, engraving and etching, and raised printing to an unparalleled level of expressive power. Only Rembrandt in European art was to approach a similar level of mastery.

Among Rembrandt's prints there are no noble series inspired by the Bible or mythology; rather his etchings take their origin from a personal need to express. Throughout his life, Rembrandt maintained a continuous interest in the depiction of light. He used a different approach in his etchings to the sudden juxtapositions of light and dark
2 found in his oil paintings. In *Abraham Francen: Apothecary* of *c.*1657, the forms at first sight appear to emerge from the shadows. By adapting the lines to describe the shadows rather than the shapes, he has given the impression of strong sunlight breaking into a connoisseur's dusty study.

While Burrell's old-master prints are few in number, the watercolours and drawings add substantially to the examples of the French School. Honoré Daumier's pen-and-wash
3 drawing, *Bons Confrères,* is a powerful indictment of the legal system in 19th-century France. The two lawyers greet each other, totally unconcerned about and untouched by the grief of the woman emerging from the law courts on the right. Daumier used the full extent of his biting satire on the legal profession. There is scarcely a drawing in this genre that does not expose its hypocrisy or

1 *Albrecht Dürer* The Death of the Virgin, *1510, woodcut* *31.7×23.5cm (12½×9¼in).*

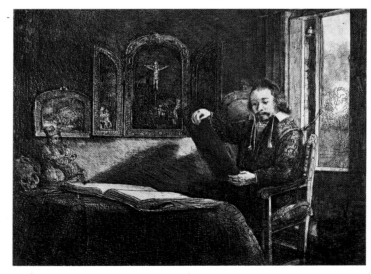

2 *Rembrandt van Rijn* Abraham Francen: Apothecary, *c.1657, etching* *17.8×21.6cm (7×8½in).*

3 *Honoré Daumier* **Bons Confrères**, *pen and wash 26×33.6cm (10¼×13¼in).*

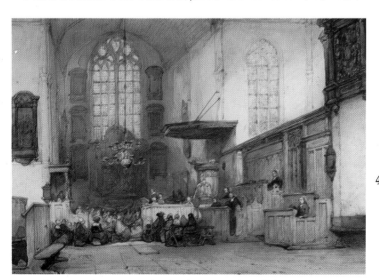

4 *Johannes Bosboom* De Kerk, Vlasslin, *watercolour, 27.3×36.8cm (10¾×14½in).*

rapacious greed. As Daumier draws them, there is a sinister aspect to the lawyers, but it is counterbalanced by a comic sense that

makes them seem preposterous rather than evil. Daumier's political views and social conscience were expressed in his graphic art rather than his oil paintings and led to a term of imprisonment in 1832 for a caricature he published of King Louis Philippe.

In Holland, Daumier's contemporary, Johannes Bosboom (1817-91), was producing less radical pictures. His art had a strong element of the 17th-century Dutch tradition, inspired principally by the church interiors of
4 Emanuel de Witte. *De Kerk, Vlasslin* is a typical product of Bosboom's style, showing his fluid washes and calligraphic lines which were to be so influential on the later painters of the Hague School.

That Sir William Burrell had a sense of humour is evident from his one hundred and forty seven sketches and cartoons by the Punch cartoonist Phil May (1864-1903). May's drawing style was developed by necessity. In 1882, he worked in Australia as a cartoonist for a newspaper whose printing presses were so erratic that he adopted a strong,

6 *Phil May* **Cartoon:** *Keeper: "I thowt yar was workin' up at Morley's farm?" Giles: "Well, so I wer' but two weeks ago t'owd cow died, an' we' ad to eat 'un. And t'next week, t'sow died, and we 'ad to eat 'un. And this morning t'gaffer's mother-in-law died. So I thowt I'd leave."*
Pen and ink 27.6×20.3cm (10⅞×8in).

6 simple line to ensure that his work would reproduce well. This cartoon illustrates his reserved style where only the essential details are included, in this case to suggest a rural background. Although he received no training in art, May's work shows a high degree of technical accomplishment.

Sir William Burrell could not claim to be a patron of contemporary artists except in one instance, his acquisition of works by Joseph Crawhall (1861-1913). Sir William identified to such an extent with Crawhall's watercolours that they offer an insight into his tastes in art.

Joseph Crawhall is traditionally grouped with the artists known as the Glasgow Boys. These artists – James Guthrie, E. A. Walton, John Lavery and George Henry among others – worked in and around Glasgow during the period 1880-90. They reacted against the highly detailed and minutely finished anecdotal pictures then so fashionable. Instead, they believed that art should be about light, colour, design and composition – qualities which are the essence of Crawhall's work.

5 *Joseph Crawhall* **The Chinese Goose,** *watercolour on linen 30.4×37.4cm (12×14¾in).*

156

Born at Morpeth near Newcastle in 1861, Crawhall worked in Scotland with the Glasgow Boys until the period 1884-93 7 when he travelled frequently to Tangier in Morocco and to Spain. The last years of his life were spent in Yorkshire.

A technically brilliant and inventive watercolourist Crawhall reflects in his works the fascination and love he had for all animals and birds. Through patient observation, with superb draughtsmanship and obvious humour, he captures their appearance and character. As Sir John Lavery wrote "No artist I have known could say more with fewer brushstrokes."

Although Crawhall's artistic career spanned thirty five years he was not a prolific artist and only about four hundred surviving works are known, many of which are the slightest sketches. During the artist's lifetime collectors vied with each other to purchase his works. The Burrell Collection contains some hundred and forty watercolours, gouaches and sketches making it the largest and finest collection in existence; a fitting testimony to the skill Sir William devoted to seeking out and acquiring works by Crawhall over a seventy year period.

7 *Joseph Crawhall* **An Arab Raid,** *watercolour heightened with bodycolour on paper, 29.6×41.3cm (11×15¾in).*

Sculpture

Burrell acquired a small number of bronzes by 19th and 20th-century sculptors, which complement the themes that appealed to him in pictures. *The Blacksmith* by Constantin Meunier (1831-1905) is an exercise in social realism in a vein similar to the paintings of the French Realists. It is a reduction of one of Meunier's principal works, also known by the title of *The Hammerman*. A Belgian, Meunier found his subjects principally among miners, factory workers and stevedores, and his theme was the heroism and nobility of labour. For the Realists, the blacksmith became a particularly symbolic figure. He was considered to be an artisan who retained his individuality by using ancient methods, so acting as a challenge to the machinery and industrialization which the Realists saw as having a malevolent and depressing influence on people's lives.

The Collection is fortunate in possessing fourteen bronzes by Auguste Rodin (1840-1917). Rodin died in the same year as Degas, and the two are often associated because of their mutual concern for interesting and arresting forms and their outstanding technical ability, which are what appealed to Burrell.

Although Rodin came from a humble background, he became highly cultured and deeply read, as the allusions in his work suggest. In the same way that Degas concentrated on a few themes so as to know them thoroughly, Rodin concentrated on the human body. He found as much beauty in the aged, sagging body of the old woman in *The Helmet-maker's Old Wife* as in the firm and supple bodies of the young.

The Thinker occupied a crowning position on Rodin's magnum opus, *The Gates of Hell*. This was a commission he had received from the French government in 1880 for a monumental portal to the School of Decorative Arts in Paris. The project was never fully assembled and completed in his lifetime because he constantly changed its design. He worked on the doors for over twenty years, but it was not until nine years after his death that they were cast for the first

1 *Constantin Meunier* The Blacksmith, *1870/80, bronze, height 48.2cm (19in).*

time. Rodin saw *The Gates of Hell* as representing Dante's *Inferno*, with *The Thinker* as the poet Dante himself, pondering the fate of mankind. The figure was intended to be seen from below, so Rodin lengthened the arms and enlarged the shoulders to give a towering and dominating effect. *The Thinker* is perhaps Rodin's best-known work, and there are many casts. This bronze is in the original size and there are another twenty-one pieces known. There are a further twelve enlarged versions, one of which was placed over Rodin's grave at his own request.

2 *Auguste Rodin* The Thinker, *1880/81, bronze, height 68.5cm (27in).*

Index